Highlights

Highlights

AN ILLUSTRATED HISTORY OF CANNABIS

A Smith Sherman Book

Ten Speed Press

Berkeley / Toronto

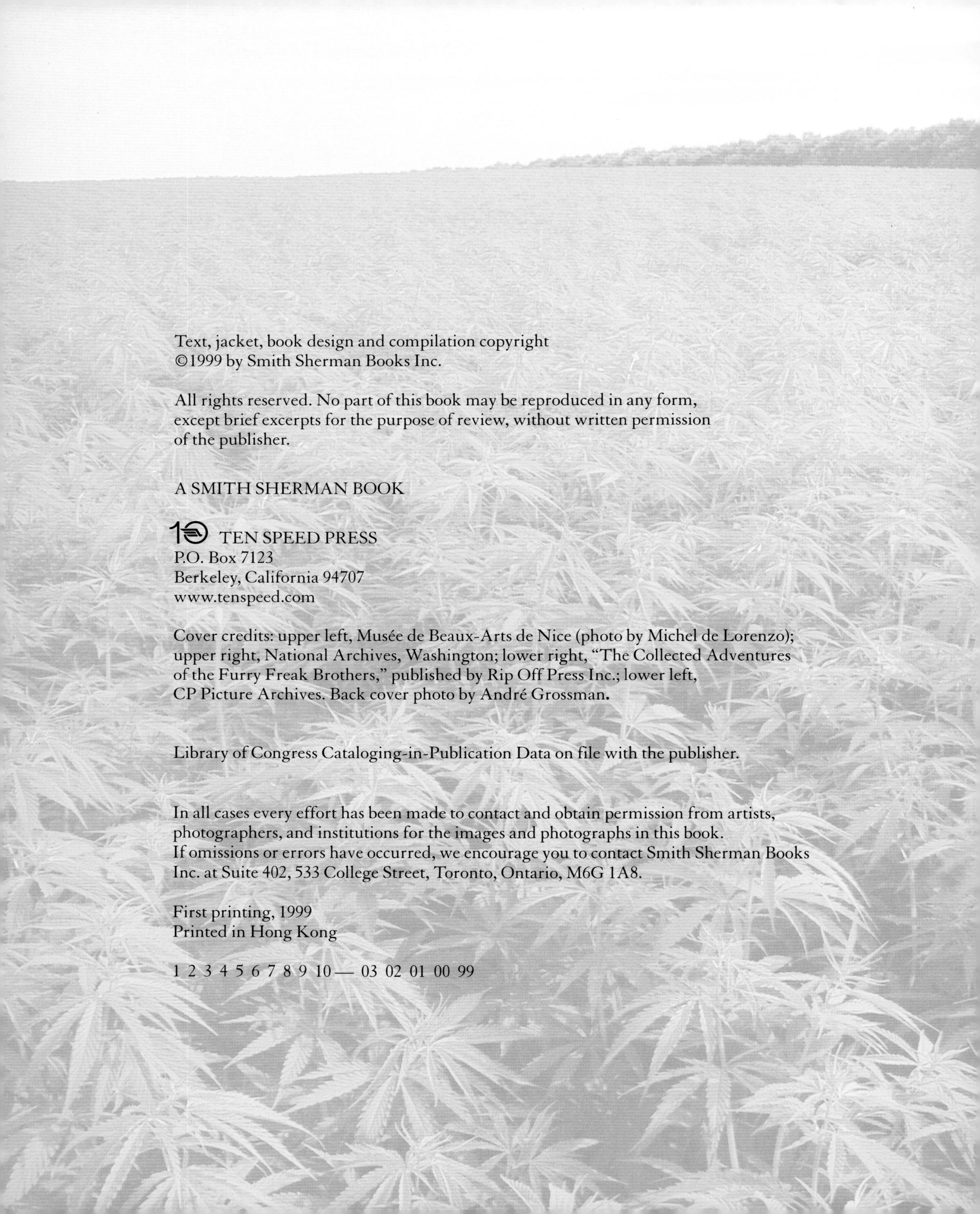

A SMITH SHERMAN BOOK

10 TEN SPEED PRESS
P.O. Box 7123
Berkeley, California 94707
www.tenspeed.com

Cover credits: upper left, Musée de Beaux-Arts de Nice (photo by Michel de Lorenzo);
upper right, National Archives, Washington; lower right, "The Collected Adventures
of the Furry Freak Brothers," published by Rip Off Press Inc.; lower left,
CP Picture Archives. Back cover photo by André Grossman.

Library of Congress Cataloging-in-Publication Data on file with the publisher.

In all cases every effort has been made to contact and obtain permission from artists,
photographers, and institutions for the images and photographs in this book.
If omissions or errors have occurred, we encourage you to contact Smith Sherman Books
Inc. at Suite 402, 533 College Street, Toronto, Ontario, M6G 1A8.

First printing, 1999
Printed in Hong Kong

1 2 3 4 5 6 7 8 9 10 — 03 02 01 00 99

"To have some hemp in your pocket."
To have luck on your side in the most adverse
circumstances. The phrase is French,
Avoir de la corde-de-pendu dans sa poche,
referring to the popular notion that hemp
brings good luck.

Brewer's Dictionary of Phrase and Fable,
originally published in 1870.

CONTENTS

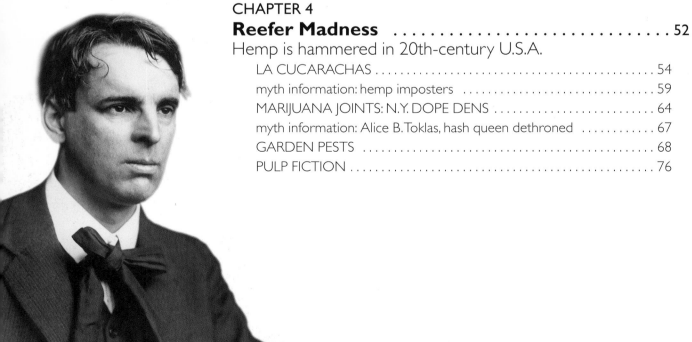

BOWEN ISLAND
BREWING
Co. Ltd.
+688333
341 ml
Keep Refrigerated
4.5% alc./vol.
O.G. 1044
ORIGINAL
Hemp Cream Ale
Brewed At The Bowen Island Brewing Co. Ltd. Vancouver, British Columbia, Canada. www.bowenbrewing.com

Foreword

SOMETHING FUNNY is in the air.

A pop-culture artifact from the 1960s and 1970s is making a remarkable comeback. More than a comeback, in fact; once feared and loathed in genteel circles, this curious plant is primed for respectability. For a while, it was all the buzz, a rallying point for the counterculture, the scourge of squares and the hero of the hip and the hippie. Smoke. Weed. The greeny green. Hey, man, cannabis is back in a big way.

Whether puffed, but not always inhaled, by presidents, or smoked by teenage hippie wannabes, or woven into hemp fabrics to make ecotrendy

"I began to gather the leaves of this plant and to eat them, and they have produced in me the gaiety that you witness. Come with me, then, that I may teach you to know it." *Haydar, an ascetic monk, describing his discovery of cannabis in 13th-century Persia. From* Tales of Hashish, *edited by Andrew C. Kimmens.*

sports coats and those goofy tea-cozy hats, or prescribed by doctors to relieve everything from constipation to cancer, cannabis is making a name for itself.

The purple and reddish leaves of a marijuana hybrid (opposite), named "Kush," indicate it was cultivated in a cold climate.

Some may be shocked by pot's popularity. After alcohol and tobacco, illegal pot is the Western world's most favorite recreational drug. According to the United States Department of Health and Human Services, seventy million Americans have smoked the herb at some point in their lives, while some ten million get high on a regular basis. Pot's also big business: the annual illegal cannabis crop grosses tens of billions of dollars. At the same time the war on cannabis continues. Today, it's still illegal to grow, buy, possess, or smoke marijuana in most countries in the world, and anyone caught breaking the rules could spend time in prison, where, by the way, pot use is rampant. In fact, there are more marijuana criminals languishing in jails today than at any other point in Western history.

Nevertheless, governments around the world are allowing farmers

Hempe.

‡ 2 Cannabis fœmina.
Femeline, or Female Hempe.

to grow hemp and doctors to experiment with high-potency cannabis. So far in the U.S., thirty-five states have passed medical marijuana laws, giving permission for doctors to test or prescribe pot for therapeutic use. Great Britain is allowing doctors to investigate the medical uses of marijuana. At the same time, Germany, England, Canada, and more than twenty countries now grow industrial hemp.

So it's high time we took stock of our cannabis culture. It's high time, in other words, for *Highlights*, a book that looks at the cannabis carousel, and tries to figure out where we are and how we got here.

Just a word of caution: here's what this book isn't. It's not a plaintive plea for the legalization of marijuana, nor a two-thumbs-up endorsement of current laws. It's also not a relentless attack on the moral decay of the modern world, as personified by those who would smoke, eat, grow, prescribe, or wear the weed. On the morality of marijuana, then, *Highlights* strives to be as neutral as Queen Elizabeth's color sense. Instead, the book looks at the ebb and flow of history, the forces that have brought cannabis in and out of favor in the West and around the world. It's a confusing story, made hazier by the smoky distortions and pure BS being pushed as Truth by both sides of the cannabis debate.

Even terms like "cannabis," "marijuana," and "hemp" are politically charged and can be misleading. We keep things simple in this book. "Cannabis" serves as the all-purpose word for the group of plants in the *Cannabis* family, including *Cannabis sativa*, the most common form, and — for those budding know-it-alls — the lesser-known *Cannabis indica* and *Cannabis ruderalis*. "Marijuana" refers to the dried flowers of the female cannabis plant that is used as an intoxicant. "Hashish" is the concentrated resin that develops on the female flowers and is the strongest cannabis around. "Hemp" means cannabis grown for industrial purposes. *Highlights* is a sampling of cannabis history, an attempt to compress ten thousand years into one easily digestible chunk.

It's been a long, strange trip for cannabis, and along the way this wily weed has been deified and demonized, banned and bandied about to the point that it's hard to know when the truth ends and the marijuana myth begins. So sit back, relax, and enjoy the biography of the most fascinating plant in human history.

"Fragrant smoke from the Arabian plant's brown juice creates a swirling dance of powerful fantasies."

Illustration and quote from the German book of poems, Album von Radirungen, *by Moritz von Schwind (1875).*

Many famous artists, including Vincent van Gogh, painted on canvases made from cannabis. In the 8th century, an unknown Japanese artist created this painting of Kichijo-ten, Goddess of Good Fortune, on a strip of hemp cloth.

CHAPTER ONE

Grass Roots

CANNABIS IN ANCIENT TIMES

IT'S HARD TO imagine how a simple weed could attract so much attention. But the plucky *Cannabis sativa* plant has kept itself in the public eye for millennia. Humans have found countless ways to put this versatile plant to work. We use the stalk to make hemp, one of the most durable and enduring fibers the world has ever encountered. In the flowers, we find an intriguing chemical, tetrahydrocannabinol or THC, a favorite of priests, doctors, and

"According to an old legend, a Japanese girl from a simple family fastened the end of a ball of hemp to the garment of her secret lover when he bade her good-bye. The thread led her to the temple of Miva, and thus revealed the divine origin of the stranger."

An ancient Japanese fable.

party animals since the dawn of time. We also crush the seeds to make hemp oil, an ingredient not uncommon in a range of household products, such as soap, paint, and varnish.

The plant itself is nothing special to look at. Its serrated leaves are distinctive, but hardly beautiful. Growing anywhere from a few inches in height — perfect for life under the basement hot lights — to as high as an elephant's eye, the cannabis plant is comfortable in a range of climates and locales, and can be found almost everywhere on the planet, far from the Central Asian plains where the plant probably originated.

This 300-year-old lacquerware comb with its distinctive marijuana leaf motif came from the household of a wealthy Japanese merchant.

Cannabis roots run deep in human history. As long as humans have been tilling the earth, they've been cultivating a special relationship with cannabis. In fact, some scientists think that cannabis was the first crop our ancestors turned to when they moved from hunters and gatherers to farmers. Archeologists have found evidence of cannabis in prehistoric Asian pottery

— one finding from Taiwan dates back ten thousand years — while modern-day primitives, like the pygmy hunters of the Congo, cultivate cannabis, a practice they say dates back to the beginning of time.

Cannabis advocates point to the plant's long history as a kind of grandfather clause justification for its modern-day acceptance. It's fractured logic, of course. Cannibalism, beheadings, and poor dental hygiene have been prevalent at various points and places in history, but that's no reason to turn to them now. What is interesting, though, is the difference between those ancient civilizations which embraced cannabis as an intoxicant and those that largely ignored it. Expansionist empires like those of the Assyrians, Romans, and, to a lesser extent, the Greeks had little time for cannabis. Alcohol was their drug of choice, and there's little doubt why. To realize their dreams of conquest, these empires had to keep the rabble loud and rowdy. Rome wasn't built in a day, and the empire may have never seen the light of day if the army had consisted of grinning potheads instead of legions of ace warriors nursing vicious red wine hangovers.

Prince Siddhartha, later known as Buddha, was said to have eaten only hemp seeds for the six years before his enlightenment.

That's not to say that these cultures didn't know about cannabis. Certainly, the Greeks and Romans used hemp fiber for making rope and fabric, and occasionally ingested cannabis for medicinal purposes. But as a recreational drug, it never gained the kind of widespread acceptance in the classical world that it enjoyed in more sedentary civilizations.

The earliest known reference to cannabis speaks of its medical significance, although people were no doubt already aware of its recreational and ritual value. The legendary Chinese emperor and physician, Shen Nung, who lived around 2300 B.C.E., made the first recorded references to cannabis. He recommended doctors use a hemp elixir to treat patients with everything from constipation and menstrual cramps to postpartum depression and gout. Shen called cannabis one of the Superior Elixirs of Immortality.

In time, hemp gained so much prominence as the venerated mulberry plant (the food of silkworms) that the ancients referred to China as the Land of Mulberry and Hemp. Since prehistory, cannabis was a staple of the Chinese economy, providing the key ingredient for everything from clothing and footwear to baskets and laquerware. Despite its abundance, cannabis never caught on as an intoxicant in China. The earliest religious records show that Chinese priests tended to look down on cannabis. According to author Ernest Abel's *Marihuana: The First Twelve Thousand Years*, around 600 B.C.E. the early Taoists dismissed the herb as a manifestation of yin, the negative, passive female life force. Marijuana weakened the body and the senses and was to be avoided in favor of manly, invigorating yang food and drink, the ancient Chinese equivalent of steak and beer. In time, however, the Taoists recognized the intoxicating effects of cannabis, and began to use it in incense, which they said would help devotees achieve visionary states.

The people of Japan, like the Chinese, valued cannabis first and foremost as a fiber. Highly regarded for its durability and flexibility, hemp, also known as *asa*, stood at the very top of the pantheon of Japanese fibers. The Japanese considered hemp a symbol of purity, and made it the fiber of choice

mythinformation

HOLY SMOKES

The closest the Bible comes to cannabis is the Gutenberg Bible (left), which was printed on hemp in the 15th century. Despite claims by the Rastas and other hopefuls, there is little evidence that the Bible gives its blessings specifically for cannabis use. However, it does take a generally favorable view toward the moderate use of intoxicants, and nowhere prohibits their use.

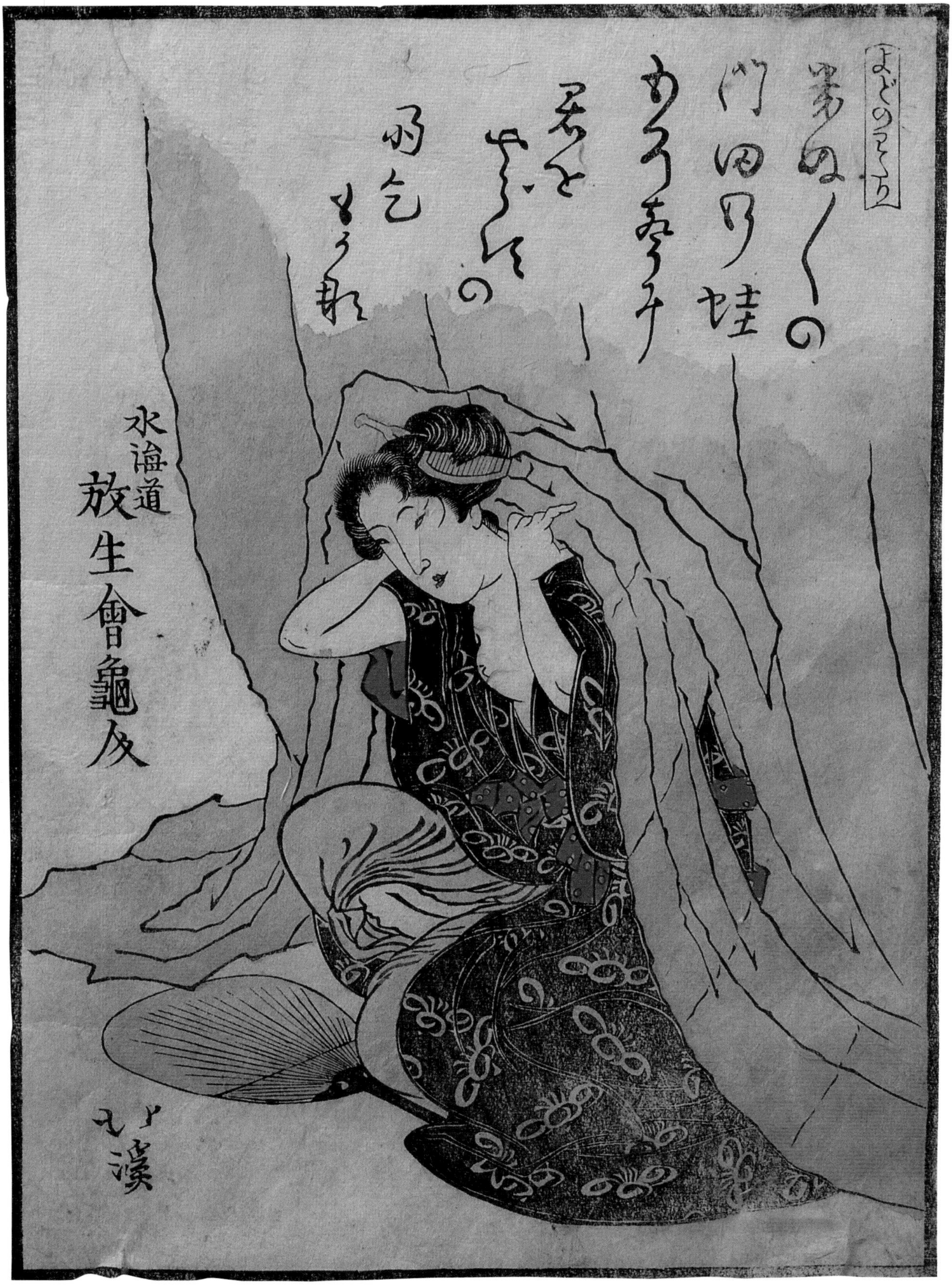
水海道
放生會龜及

for religious and ceremonial garb. The plant was particularly associated with love and marriage: newlyweds were often given gifts of hemp, which reflected the strength of their bond. Meanwhile, brides traditionally dressed in hemp cloth to indicate that they would be pliable and obedient, just like hemp fiber. Because of its perceived purity, hemp played an important role in traditional Japanese medicine. Shinto priests would bang hemp rods on a patient's bed to ward off the evil spirits.

Other ancient civilizations may have flirted with cannabis, but India embraced it with open arms. Both Hindus and Buddhists revered the plant's intoxicating effects, and made it an important part of the day-to-day ritual and routine. It is said that during his six years of meditation leading to his enlightenment, the Buddha ate only hemp seeds. Meanwhile, Hindus can read about cannabis in their most holy book, the *Vedas*, and associate the weed with the highest gods of their religion. God Shiva and his wife Kali-Ma, the Mother of Life and Death, are closely associated to marijuana or, as it was known there, *bhang*, a potent pot potable made with hot milk and eleven different herbs and spices. Shiva, aka Lord of the Bhang, a recent nickname and takeoff of his more established title, Lord of the Dance, is often credited with giving the gift of cannabis to the Indian people. Kali worshippers are renowned for their Tantric ceremonies which feature both ritual sex and the use of *bhang*. The goal of the Tantra initiate was to achieve unity of mind, body, and spirit through yoga and marathon sexual episodes. These were fueled by *bhang*, which heightens the sexual experience.

Bhang eventually worked its way into almost every aspect of Indian life. Similar to booze in the West, *bhang* was, and remains, an integral part of social gatherings. Cannabis is so prevalent, in fact, that Indians have developed three levels of potency: mild *bhang*, which gives you a mild bang; medium, or *ganja*, made from cannabis leaves and flowers; and extra-spicy *charas*, made only from the finest dew-picked, resin-covered flower tops, and about as potent as pure hashish. *Charas* was favored by fakirs, semi-masochistic holy men famous for walking on hot coals and sleeping on beds of nails, who believed that the herb put them in closer communion with their gods.

Why was marijuana such a popular part of Indian life? For one thing,

"Lady emerges from her moskito (sic) net," (opposite) by Hokkei. Mosquito nets made from hemp have been in use since medieval times and are still in use today.

India's semi-arid climate is perfect for cannabis, so the plant grew in abundance in the region; in the hot sun, cannabis sweats out its hallucinogenic resin, which covers the flowers and leaves in a protective layer, and can provide even the poorest passerby with a Grade A high. Meanwhile, the raw ingredients for other intoxicants — poppies for opium, grains for spirits and beer, grapes for wine — were harder to come by. But the actual effect of the herb was also significant. India has had a tumultuous history. Poverty, over-crowding, disease, and civil strife were common. Many people turned to *bhang* and its cannabis cousins to find a kind of inner solace that wasn't available in the everyday world. At the same time, unlike opium users, who tend to withdraw, or drinkers, whose behavior can be violent and unpredictable, cannabis users remain fairly amicable and would not disrupt India's close-knit, and crowded, social structure.

THE BIG BHANG

India has a long history of cannabis use. And not just by mystics to open the doors of perception. In the Tantric religion, which developed in Tibet in the 7th century, initiates used drugs to achieve unity of mind, body, and spirit through yoga and marathon sexual episodes. These lusty pursuits were fueled by *bhang*, a liquid mixture of marijuana leaves, milk, and spices, said to heighten the sexual experience. In the 1750 painting (opposite), the lovers are in a palace pavilion with the ubiquitous hookah and their hashish.

While marijuana grew on the people of India, the Arab world was developing a cannabis culture of its own, one with repercussions that are felt today in the Western world. Although not universally enjoyed by the Moslem people, cannabis in its most potent form — hashish — played an important role in the history and traditions of specific groups. Sufis are an ancient breakaway Moslem group, whose founder, Haydar, is said to have been the first to discover the uplifting powers of the plant. Sometime in the tenth century, Haydar, an ascetic monk, went out for a walk and discovered a cannabis plant standing tall and florid in the withering afternoon sun. Curious to know how the plant beat the heat, Haydar snipped off a couple of leaves and munched away while he finished his walk. When he arrived back at the monastery hours later, the usually laconic Haydar was uncharacteristically

18

talkative. His disciples realized that this indeed was a wondrous plant. In time, Haydar and his followers developed a mystical discipline which centered around self-denial and hashish. Ernest Abel called them "the hippies of the Arab world," who, like the Flower Children of the 1960s, "rejected the dominant economic system in favor of communal living." Thanks to a loophole in the Moslem holy text, the Koran, which banned the use of alcohol but failed to mention cannabis, the Sufis maintained that spiritual enlightenment could be obtained by experiencing altered states of consciousness, and came to honor hashish as a sacrament. It's not surprising that within the rigid Arab social structure, which valued conformity, Sufis were

"They get no usefulness from this, unless it is in the fact that they become ravished by ecstasy, and delivered from all worries and cares, and laugh at the least little thing." *Dr. Garcia Da Orta on the Indians' use of* bhang *in 1534. From* Tales of Hashish, *edited by Andrew C. Kimmens.*

mistrusted, despised, and persecuted, and left on the losing end of the first recorded war on drugs. Launched around 1250, it would make a modern drug enforcement agent green with envy. Penalties for possession were dismemberment or simple execution.

Around the same time, another group was banding behind a charismatic Moslem ascetic named Hasan. Known in legend and lore as the Assassins, this group began a hard-sell public relations campaign which featured executions for anyone who spoke out against them. The Assassins were associated with hashish, which, it was said, they consumed in great quantities to bolster their courage. It was more guilt by association than anything else. Medieval Arabs generally frowned on drug use; the upper class considered it a low-class vice, and to accuse someone of hashish use was the greatest of insults. In any case, tall tales of the Assassins eventually filtered from the Arab world westward, igniting the fantasies, fears, and fascination of Christian civilization.

Shiva, an Indian deity shown here with his family (opposite), is often credited with giving the gift of cannabis to the Indian people.

ROPE vs dope

You can make it into paper and rope, or roll it into an intoxicating cigarette. How can one plant be so many things to so many people?

Anyone who's ever looked at a seed catalogue knows how one plant from the same family can have many different varieties — whether it's tomatoes, roses, or cannabis.

Historically, the astute farmer who grew cannabis for hemp to make rope gathered only seeds from plants that had grown tall and hardy. Eventually, over many seasons, the farmer's crop would be consistently tall and have a more bountiful yield. Today, farmers that are licensed to grow hemp use special government-approved seeds that have had THC, the psychoactive chemical that gets you high, almost bred out of it. These low THC seeds go into the ground and, all things being normal, would produce a crop of hemp. A few years ago, however, when weather conditions were hotter and drier than usual, plants grown from these seeds developed levels of unacceptably high THC. The farmers, through no fault of their own, could have been arrested and had their farms confiscated.

On the other hand the farmer who grows cannabis for marijuana breeds a plant with high levels of THC. Indeed, breeding for this purpose has become a secret science that is flourishing in attics, closets, and basements all over the world. There are seeds developed specifically for life indoors under electric lights. There are seeds for every climate zone. Seeds bred to be resistant to mold that grow well in a swamp or at the side of a river. Early budding seeds are preferred in northern climates and mountainous regions. There was a time when marijuana growers favored a tall plant, because of the yield. Now illegal outdoor growers prefer a variety that is potent, but short, to avoid discovery.

Two varieties of cannabis produce two very different crops. A field of hemp-producing cannabis (top) is grown for its long fibrous stems, and a patch of lush, bushy cannabis (below) will yield a rich bounty of buds for somebody's smoking pleasure.

Trouillebert

CHAPTER TWO

Go West Young Weed

THE 15th CENTURY AND BEYOND

CANNABIS FIRST ENTERED the popular imagination of the Western world thanks to the stories of the adventurer and merchant, Marco Polo. His *Book of Ser Marco Polo*, detailing his travels through the Arab world, was widely read in the fourteenth century. In his book, Polo told lurid tales of Hasan and his Assassins, and described how they fueled their murderous orgies with hashish. Not unfamiliar with the drug thanks to firsthand reports from veterans of the Crusades, Europeans easily accepted the vision of hashish as a

La Servante de Harem (*1874, opposite*), *by Paul-Désiré Trouillebert* (*also see page 26*).

"Not being used to hashish...he burst into extraordinary hilarity and filled the hall with shouts of laughter. A moment later he collapsed backward onto the marble floor and fell prey to hallucinations."

The Arabian Nights, *"The Tale of the Hashish Eater" (10th century).*

dangerous concoction, which was rumored to turn even the lowest infidel into a murderous fiend with superhuman powers. And so, cannabis started off on the wrong foot in the West.

Although cannabis entered the Western mind relatively recently, some pro-cannabis commentators have tried to establish much older links. They pour through the Old Testament and other ancient texts to find references to the weed in hopes of establishing some kind of biblical authority for its use. The results are tenuous at best: a few vague references in the Song of Solomon; some unsubstantiated and unlikely claims that Christmas originated as a Hemp God Festival. The fact is that cannabis played no significant part in pre-Christian and Christian traditions. The Jewish authors of the Bible came from a nomadic background, which

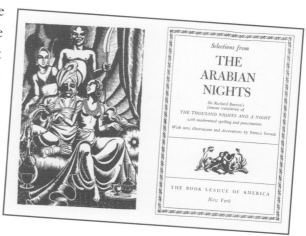

Selections from
THE
ARABIAN
NIGHTS
Sir Richard Burton's famous translation of
THE THOUSAND NIGHTS AND A NIGHT
with modernized spelling and punctuation.
With new illustrations and decorations by STEELE SAVAGE
THE BOOK LEAGUE OF AMERICA
New York

has never been conducive to cannabis consumption. Meanwhile, grapes grew in abundance in the region, and early Jews and Christians alike developed a fondness for wine, which became the intoxicant of choice for ceremonies and celebrations. It's an important point that's overlooked by those looking to build a positive case for cannabis, many of whom like to blame Christianity for contemporary prohibitions against the weed. However, the Bible takes a generally favorable view toward the moderate use of intoxicants, and nowhere specifically prohibits their use.

Cannabis as an intoxicant played little part in Western tradition, but the

THE ORIENT EXPRESSION

Artists from all over Europe flocked to the exotic, remote world of North Africa and the Near East in the wake of Napoleon's Egyptian campaign in 1798. The Oriental experience had a powerful influence on important painters such as Delacroix, Renoir, and Matisse, who were intrigued by the ancient culture and the effect of the sun's intense light on shadow and color. Painted scenes from the Orient were extremely popular during the 19th century in Europe and in many instances they informed the Western mind about dope smoking. In Paul-Désiré Trouillebert's *La Servante de Harem* (page 24), a sullen-gazing slave carries an ornate hookah with a gigantic chunk of hashish in the pipe's bowl. The combination of naked women and dope smoking not only sparked the erotic imagination but challenged existing conventions. As in Jean-Léon Gérôme's *Allumeuse de Narghilé* (opposite), a woman stokes up some hashish while taking it easy poolside.

plant itself, in its hemp incarnation, had a long and noble history in Europe. In Germany, archeologists have found evidence of hemp dating back more than twenty-five hundred years, and there's hardly a region on the continent where the plant wasn't grown. The Vikings used hemp rigging on their pleasure and plunder cruises, and hemp clothing was all the rage among the fashionable barbarians of Paris and Milan. Hemp really came into its own as the Middle Ages gave way to the Renaissance, and shipping became the backbone of the economy; transportation, communication, and trade all depended on ships, and outside of wood, hemp was the raw material that kept the industry going. Ropes and riggings, sails, even the shirts off the sailors' backs, were all made from hemp, a durable fiber that resisted the corrosive influence of salt water. In the earliest days, Italian ports, most notably Venice, that venerable center of Mediterranean trade, were the most important hemp hot spots. Venice even had a hemp guild, an association of craftsmen devoted to producing the highest quality of hemp materials.

Hemp on the High Seas

Hemp cultivation and its importation was serious business in 16th-century England and remained so until the late 19th century. During the Tudor period, the British navy depended on hemp for rope and canvas sails to such a degree that a Royal proclamation decreed a fine be levied on English farmers who did not grow it. A first-rate man-of-war required 80 tons of rough hemp to supply her with the necessary tackle. The vessels shown here from the painting *English Ships and the Spanish Armada* (1588) would have collectively required one good hemp crop grown on a minimum of 10,000 acres to make the rigging needed for them to be properly outfitted.

George Washington (opposite), president, passionate gardener, and hemp farmer, is depicted here in a 17th-century lithograph by Claude Regnier.

In time, as maritime fortunes shifted, the demand for hemp in England outstripped the needs of the rest of Europe combined and, in the process, added to some of the plant's negative PR. King Henry VIII was heads above previous British monarchs when it came to recognizing the value of hemp, and in 1563 he ordered farmers to each devote a small portion of their soil to growing hemp. But the farmers were reluctant to follow Henry's orders. For one thing, the plant brought them a relatively low return at the market. Besides, the farmers believed that the hemp plant sucked all the nutrients out of the soil, leaving it barren for other crops. Farmers by and large ignored the edict, and continued to ignore it thirty years later, when Henry's daughter Queen Elizabeth I issued it again. Eventually, the Crown gave up. By the end of the seventeenth century, England had repealed her mandatory cultivation laws, and the country was importing nearly all the fiber it needed for both its maritime and linen industries from Russia. This left the country vulnerable to outside forces; an enemy could cripple England simply by cutting off its hemp supply. Meanwhile, the whole hemp experience left a bad taste in the collective mouth of the common people. They'd come to resent the way that hemp imposed itself on their lives, and how England's dependence on the fiber had become its Achilles' heel.

While hemp was near and dear to the commercial heart of Europe, its intoxicating effects did not go unnoticed. In some regions, particularly Eastern

mythinformation

PRESIDENTIAL POTHEADS?

There is much speculation that George Washington, who we definitely know grew hemp, also got high. Much is made about his diary entries where he laments the fact that he didn't separate the males from the females before fertilization. Because the female marijuana plant is the one to grow for intoxicating effects, and has to be separated from the male, many point to this as evidence that he got high. However, as Larry Sloman points out in *Reefer Madness,* "Separating the male from the female is flimsy evidence that Washington desired a resin-soaked female plant for personal recreational or medicinal use. In all likelihood, he was stashing the strong fibrous male plants and discarding the psychoactive females."

Europe where the plant grew freely, cannabis formed the base of many folk medicine remedies. Peasants prescribed cannabis for everything from toothaches — they believed the drug would put to sleep the worms that caused the pain — and childbirth to arthritis and epilepsy. Meanwhile, in Central Europe cannabis found its way into the ritual world of witchcraft and sorcery, and in 1484, cannabis was dealt one more public relations blow when Pope Innocent VIII forbade the ritual use of hemp as part of a general attack on satanic masses. What the modern reader has to remember is that these masses were the central ritual in what writer Émile Grillot de Givry referred to as "The Church of Evil," an underground movement that sys-

"Hemp is abundantly productive and will grow forever on the same spot. But the breaking and beating it, which has always been done by hand, is so slow, so laborious, and so much complained of by our laborers, that I have given it up."

From Thomas Jefferson's Farm Book, *edited by E. M. Betts.*

tematically challenged the spiritual authority of the Catholic church. Across Europe, men and women who felt alienated by the opulence of God's church decided to cast their lot with Satan. Every ceremony in the anti-Church was a conscious parody of Christian ritual, and when it came time to mock the use of wine in Holy Communion, cannabis won out by default. It offered a cheap high, which even in small doses gave a sense of spiritual, not to mention sexual, ecstasy that made the ornate trappings of the Catholic church seem pointless. For impoverished medieval devil worshippers, pot was a godsend, but their love of the drug earned a heap of bad press that cannabis was never able to completely live down.

As the European empires moved to the New World, they took their hemp with them. The earliest settlers in North America were contracted to grow hemp in exchange for safe passage to the New World. The early Puritans, of all people, grew *Cannabis sativa* in abundance, yielding high-quality hemp. To many hempsters, this mocks current laws restricting production of the plant; if the notoriously pious Puritans could grow it, the argument runs, why can't the modern American farmer? However, the Jamestown settlers did not want to grow it, and only did so under pressure from their corporate sponsors, the Virginia Company. The Puritans preferred growing tobacco, which had a much greater profit margin. Likewise, France encouraged early settlers in Quebec to also grow cannabis for the shipping industry back home.

Hemp earned the resentment of early settlers, but it soon became one of the most important crops in the budding republic. In fact, it's safe to say that there would have never been a good old U.S. of A. if it hadn't been for hemp. By the time the first shots were fired in Lexington, in 1775, the U.S. had become self-sufficient in both the production and processing of hemp. The Thirteen Colonies were dotted with ropewalks, intricate hempworks where the fibers were twisted into thick rope; every coastal town had its ropewalk, and Boston alone had fourteen. The domestic industry had been helped by the economic crisis back in England, which saw the bottom drop out of the hemp and linen industries. In re-sponse, hundreds of Irish weavers and rope makers up and moved to the colonies. This influx of skilled labor, combined with the bounty of raw material, proved an unbeatable combination, and directly and indi-rectly supplied the revolutionary forces with everything to help win the war. Hemp went into ropes and riggings and sails for the merchant marines and clothes for the armies.

Thomas Jefferson, president and hemp farmer, shown here as Minister to France (1784 to 1789) in a woodcut by Charles Turzak.

And what hemp the revolutionaries didn't use for themselves, they sold to raise money to buy guns and cannons and bullets. By the time the British surrendered at Yorktown in 1781, hemp was considered a homegrown hero. Thomas Jefferson, George Washington, and other Founding Fathers praised hemp, and made it an important crop in their own fields. But the glory was short-lived, and in barely a century hemp fell from its place as the patron plant of patriots to international pariah, without ever doing anything wrong. Was it simply a case of being the wrong weed at the wrong time, or did other forces conspire to put pot on the back burner?

A Soldier's Story

Napoleon Bonaparte in Egypt (left) celebrates the prophet Mohammed's birthday in an engraving by A. Colin (18th century). The Little Emperor and his army were stranded in Egypt in 1798 just long enough for the troops to acquire a taste for a local delicacy — hashish. The soldiers brought their cannabis passion home with them and introduced it to France, a scenario which would be repeated 170 years later when Vietnam vets returned to the U.S.A. with shattered spirits and a newly honed taste for drugs.

Charles Baudelaire, the French writer and sometime artist, met with other members of the Club de Hashishins once a month. This self-portrait (above) is reputed to have been painted while he was high on hashish.

CHAPTER THREE

High Society

IN THE 19th CENTURY HASH IS HOT IN FRANCE AND ENGLAND

CANNABIS STARTED OFF the nineteenth century on a roll. Hemp was a hit in most countries interested in developing its economy through international trade. At the same time, cannabis was beginning to earn a reputation in the West as a powerful, if not an overpowering, drug. Physicians had been aware of the medicinal and mind-bending power of pot since at least 1563, when the Portuguese medic Garcia Da Orta wrote about the drug in his *Colloquies on the Simples and Drugs of India*. Not only did he explore some of the

"Do not dare venture such an experience if you have some disagreeable business to conclude, if your mood is exceptionally dark or if you have bills to pay." *Advice from Charles Baudelaire on the sampling of "hasheesh."*

popular medicinal uses for cannabis, but detailed firsthand accounts from drug users themselves, decorating the stories with lurid gossip of horny, cannabis-crazed women and stoned suitors.

On the eve of the nineteenth century, two seemingly unrelated events took place, which together sealed pot's fate for the next one hundred years and laid the groundwork for our modern-day marijuana prohibition. In 1798, the British East India Company went broke; that same year, Napoleon's armies invaded Egypt. The first event was important because it brought cannabis-as-drug to the public eye in Europe. The British Parliament was forced to bail out the once-flourishing company, and in an effort to recoup its losses, the Crown decided to impose a tax, which came to be known as the Indian Hemp Tax, on certain Indian industries, including those involved with the production and refinement of

In The Hasheesh Smokers, *an 1845 lithograph by Honoré Daumier, two tokers compare their experience.*

OH! WHAT AN ORIENTAL PLEASURE. I FEEL AS IF I'M TROTTING ON A CAMEL!
AND ME . . . I FEEL LIKE I'M BEING BEATEN WITH A STICK!

the cannabis-based drugs *bhang*, *ganja*, and *charas*. In the debate that followed, the government defended the tax — a callous attempt to extort money from its impoverished colony — by saying it was in India's best interests. The argument had some support, predominantly from the ruling class. Crime, madness, and social turmoil were everywhere, and *ganja* took the blame.

Why *ganja*? *Bhang* was considered a mild intoxicant, like tea or coffee, and hardly worth worrying about, while the highly refined *charas* was expensive and available only to the wealthiest members of Indian society.

"The water I was drinking seemed to have the savor of the most exquisite wine, the meat turned to raspberries in my mouth, and vice versa. I could not have told a cutlet from a peach." *Théophile Gautier,* The Hashish-Eaters Club *(1846).*

Ganja was cheap and potent, the drug of choice for India's massive masses. Many Indian leaders wanted the drug banned altogether, but the British scuttled that idea in favor of increased taxes until the cost of the drug became prohibitive. It was a theory, of course, but served its purpose: undaunted by the tax, Indians kept getting high, as the British tax revenues got higher.

Meanwhile, back in England, British doctors were turning to the drug with interest. English physicians stationed in colonial India were the first to hear stories of this wonder drug — the aspirin of its age — which could lower fevers, cure migraines, aid in digestion, induce sleep, even cure venereal disease. By the early 1800s, the drug was popular medicine in England for every imaginable ailment: epilepsy, tetanus, asthma, postpartum depression, rheumatism, gonorrhea. Even Queen Victoria jumped — well, waddled — onto the cannabis bandwagon. In a famous story, her personal physician prescribed cannabis as a treatment for severe menstrual cramps. But before you get carried away with thoughts of the grand old Queen rolling a Big Fat One, think again. The drug that her personal physician Sir Richard Reynolds prescribed was a tincture of cannabis and alcohol, and came with careful instructions. Still, Reynolds sang the praises of the drug in

The Hôtel Lauzun (opposite) aka the Hôtel Pimodan, the gathering place for the The Hashish-Eaters Club, was an old mansion on the Île Saint-Louis in Paris.

the inaugural issue of the now-celebrated medical journal *The Lancet*, writing that cannabis, "when pure and administered carefully, is one of the most valuable medicines we possess."

A ROYAL PAIN

Even Queen Victoria couldn't escape that time of the month. Her menstrual cramps were so severe that her personal physician Sir Richard Reynolds prescribed a popular medicine in England at the time — cannabis. But before you get carried away with thoughts of Victoria rolling Big Fat Ones in the palace, think again. Sir Richard's remedy was a tincture of cannabis and alcohol, and all the Queen had to do was sip it, just like tea.

One doctor in particular became an early champion of cannabis. W. B. O'Shaughnessy was first introduced to the drug, like most of us, when he went away to college. While working as an assistant professor at the Medical College of Calcutta he heard stories of this wondrous folk remedy, and began conducting experiments on dogs and other animals. He concluded from these tests that the drug would be harmless to humans, and started testing it on some patients. In 1839, he wrote the first modern medical paper on the value of cannabis, concluding that it was an excellent analgesic and "an anticonvulsive remedy of the greatest value."

O'Shaughnessy's work turned the medical community onto cannabis,

Sir William Brooke O'Shaughnessy (below), a professor of chemistry at the Medical College of Calcutta, was an early proponent of medicinal marijuana.

and soon the drug was commonly prescribed by doctors throughout Europe and North America. In the meantime, France had grown as a center for cannabis culture, all because of Napoleon's foray into Turkish-ruled Egypt. He led his troops there in 1798, in hopes of smashing Britain's trade links to the Middle East. While Egypt fell to him, Napoleon lost his fleet in the process, and he and his army were stranded in the country. During their stay, Napoleon's troops were introduced to one of the local treats, hashish, and despite the Little Emperor's strict prohibition of its use, many soldiers soon fell in love with the drug.

41

The Coffee Shop of Cairo

In 1838, David Roberts, a poor shoemaker's son and self-taught painter, hired a boat and went to Cairo. It was one of several expeditions that the English artist made, all the while drawing and recording his experiences. Roberts wrote the following about his drawing *The Coffee Shop of Cairo*, shown here as a hand-colored lithograph.

"The visitors generally bring their own pipes and tobacco, but an intoxicating preparation of hemp is often smoked, and can be obtained in the low coffee-shops; the properties of this plant were known to Galen, and even mentioned by Herodotus as used by the Scythians to produce inebriating effects. When even tactiturn Turks and Arabs become excited and boisterous in these coffee-shops it is due chiefly to the intoxicating fumes of this preparation of hemp."

The soldiers brought their newly acquired taste for cannabis home with them and introduced it to France, a scenario which would be repeated 170 years later, as Vietnam vets returned to the U.S.A. with shattered spirits and a newly honed taste for drugs. At first, hashish use was limited to a small circle of French veterans and their friends, but in time it spilled into popular culture. Again, the similarities to the U.S. in the 1960s are remarkable. Intellectuals and artists were the first to experiment with cannabis, and their interest soon trickled down to influence a generation of students.

Dr. Jacques-Joseph Moreau, a noted psychologist, spearheaded the movement. In the 1840s, Moreau began experimental cannabis treatments on mental patients, and was first impressed with the drug's positive effects; it seemed to calm the patients and relieve related problems such as headaches, appetite loss, anxiety, and sleep disorders. So in 1845 he formed the *Club de Hashishins* — "The Hash-Eaters Club" — with his friend Théophile Gautier, a writer and leading cultural figure, best known for coining the battle cry of the bohemian, "art for art's sake." The club was inspired by the

Writer W. B. Yeats (opposite) and his lover Maud Gonne (below) experimented with hashish, hoping to improve their telepathic powers.

romantic Orientalism fashionable at the time, and was dedicated to looking into the non-medicinal value of cannabis. Thanks in part to Gautier's literary connections, the *Club de Hashishins* soon became the toast of Paris. Members would arrive dressed in their finest Oriental silks, and were offered a spoonful of a greenish jelly infused with hashish. Such literary luminaries as Arthur Rimbaud, Paul Verlaine, and Charles Baudelaire were regulars at the club's once-a-month meetings, and wrote glowing reports about their drug experiences. Baudelaire, in his essay "On Wine and Hashish,"

wrote of the highs and lows of a hashish trip, with "all joy and happiness being super abundant, all sorrow and anguish immensely profound." He also cautioned against using it when you have pressing matters at hand, or are feeling down in the dumps: "Any problem or worry, any memory of work claiming your will or attention at a particular time, will sound a knell across your intoxication and poison your pleasure."

It began with the best of intentions, but the *Club de Hashishins* did more damage than good to cannabis' otherwise sterling reputation. Gautier and Baudelaire would both eventually denounce the drug, finding its effects too disturbing. "Wine makes men happy and sociable; hashish isolates them,"

"A shock, as of some unimagined vital force, shoots without warning through my entire frame, leaping to my fingers' ends, piercing my brain, startling me till I nearly spring from my chair." *Fitz Hugh Ludlow,* The Hasheesh Eater *(1856).*

Baudelaire wrote. "Wine exalts the will; hashish annihilates it." Of course, these literary dogs were eating pure hash, and if they were expecting a mild beer buzz, they were certainly barking up the wrong tree. The result was that the public came to understand the cannabis drug only in its most potent form — imagine if we only knew alcohol from the stories of people who drank 100-proof rum — and a kind of hash hysteria was born. Following his death, rumors persisted that Baudelaire had succumbed to a hashish overdose. It was syphilis that really did him in, but the damage was done. Cannabis was now the thrill *de jour*, the *de rigueur* danger of France's dilettante set.

Despite the bad press, the experimental use of cannabis extended to other Western countries, including the U.S. where Fitz Hugh Ludlow's firsthand account *The Hasheesh Eater* titillated readers, and Britain, where members of London's Rhymers Club used hashish in order to create a sense of the occult. While the Rhymers Club lacked the punch of its French counterpart — the poet and playwright W. B. Yeats was the only famous member — it did help create an image of cannabis as a drug that could be dangerous if it found its way into the wrong hands. Yeats makes some brief mentions of his "haschisch" experiences in his autobiography *The Trembling of the Veil*. He and his lover Maud Gonne are known to have experimented with hashish, hoping to improve their telepathic powers. Another Rhymer, Arthur Symons, wrote the biography about fellow Rhymer Ernest Dowson and described one afternoon when Dowson served "tea, cakes, cigarettes and then hashish."

While the Rhymers were experimenting with pot, the medical community was also busy with some testing of its own. British doctors subjected cannabis to rigorous scientific scrutiny, and more than one hundred papers were published in learned journals exploring and espousing the drug's benefits. In the U.S., cannabis was listed in the *Pharmacopoeia*, the bible of medical drug use, and free samples were even offered to visitors at the 1876 American Centennial Exhibition in Washington. Remarkably though, the drug swiftly fell from grace. Within a few years into the new century, doctors were no longer prescribing the drug, and shortly after that, governments were declaring it a dangerous drug that was unraveling the moral rolling paper of society. The old high had reached a new low. What happened?

Aubrey Beardsley illustration for The Hasheesh Eater.

They say that the grass is always greener on the other side of the fence, and that old adage is never truer than when it's applied to medical science. Doctors are always looking for more effective treatments, and today's wonder drug can quickly become yesterday's news. Such was the case of

47

A hookah-smoking caterpillar advises Alice in Lewis Carroll's Alice in Wonderland.

cannabis. Physicians stopped prescribing it, not because of some great government conspiracy, but simply out of an earnest desire to improve the quality of care for their patients.

The scientific world had always had a problem with cannabis because its effects were rather unpredictable. In part, this was because the drug is difficult to process, so the potency varied from one dose to the next. As well, each patient seemed to react differently to the drug. To a scientific community, these inconstancies were disturbing indeed. Another problem with cannabis derivatives was that, unlike opiates, they weren't water soluble, so they

"I advise any bashful young man to take hashish when he wants to offer his heart to any fair lady, for it will give him the courage of a hero, the eloquence of a poet, and the ardor of an Italian."

Dr. Meredith, a character in Louisa May Alcott's Perilous Play *(1869).*

couldn't be used in a hypodermic needle, which was invented in the 1850s. The final straw was the arrival of synthetic drugs such as aspirin, various barbiturates, and chloral hydrate, which, although arguably more harmful than cannabis, were much more chemically stable and therefore had more predictable effects on patients. All told, these developments pushed pot to the very bottom of the medical bag of tricks.

At the same time, cannabis was facing attacks on other fronts. Certainly, its reputation as a recreational drug was tainted thanks to its rejection from the members of the hashish clubs, and through the distortions the British government presented to support its Indian Hemp Tax. But the humble hemp industry was fading in the face of advancing technologies. It started with the advent of the cotton gin in 1800, which allowed for a cheaper fiber source. Over the next hundred years, sailboats gave way to steamships, and hemp was pushed further aside. Soon, the use of hemp would plummet, and as the world looked to new sources of fiber, for the first time in history people wondered if *Cannabis sativa* had anything useful to offer.

XIX b.

C F Schmidt gez u lith

A WEED
by any other name

When it comes to the origins of words in pot culture,
there are as many variations as plant varieties.
Herewith a few suggestions of where the names came from.

CANNABIS or *Cannabis sativa L.* was the name given to the hemp plant in 1753 by Swedish botanist Carolus Linnaeus. Ernest Abel, in *Marihuana: The First Twelve Thousand Years,* tells us "cannabis" comes from the Greek *kannabis*, which in turn is taken from *canna*, an early Sanskrit term. Other possible origins include *kanab* and *quonnab* (Persian); *konaba* (East Iranian); *quannab* (Celtic); *cañamo* (Spanish). In his book *Pot*, John Rosevear offers another suggestion. The Assyrians, who used hemp seeds as an incense, after breathing in the vapors, apparently made a noise to express their feelings. Their word for "noise" was *qunnabu* or *qunnubu*.

HEMP comes from the Anglo-Saxon *henep* or *haenep*. It is akin to the Dutch *henner*, Old High German *hanaf*, and the Old Norse *hampr*.

MARIJUANA origins include the Mexican generic *mariguango*, meaning "intoxicant"; or from the Mexican/Spanish slang *Maria y Juana*.

POT is slang for marijuana and there are a few suggestions where it came from. The most obvious answer is that "pot" is the shortened form of the Mexican/Spanish word *potiguaya,* which was sometimes used as a substitute for the word "marijuana." Or Rosevear suggests that old Moroccan men used to smoke their *kif* from a long pipe that they kept in a small jar, or pot. The old men sat around and smoked all day, doing nothing. People used to say, "Let him have his pipe and pot." Also Rosevear points out that in proper English the word "pot" or "potable" means drink, and possibly an intoxicating one. Hence, any substance that intoxicates was called "pot."

HASHISH, which was also spelled *hasheesh* or *haschisch* in the late 1800s and early 1900s, appears to come from Arabic, when it originally meant "herbage." It later came to mean the preparation made from cannabis. Bernard Lewis, in *The Assassins: A Radical Sect in Islam,* explains that "the use and effects of hashish were known at the time, and were no secret . . . even the name *hashīshī* (hashish eater, Assassin) is local to Syria, and is probably a term of popular abuse. In all probability it was the name that gave rise to the story, rather than the reverse." Here Lewis refers to Hasan-i-Sabbah, also known as the Old Man of the Mountains, the bad guy terrorist leader in 11th-century Persia. He and his band, known as the Assassins, executed anyone who spoke out against them. The Assassins were associated with hashish, which, it was said, they consumed in great quantities to bolster their courage.

Botanical illustration of Cannabis sativa L. from the Pharmacopoeia Borussica *(1863), by Otto Karl Berg and C. F. Schmidt, Leipzig.*

CHAPTER FOUR

Reefer Madness

HEMP IS HAMMERED IN 20th-CENTURY U.S.A.

BRITAIN AND FRANCE may have introduced cannabis to the modern world, but by the end of the nineteenth century it was the United States that was mostly responsible for hurling the drug into exile.

Of course, the climate was right for an anti-cannabis backlash. The commercial value of the plant had fallen considerably since the heyday of hemp fiber, while the popular imagination was full of hash-eater horror stories. The American experience did nothing to bolster the image of

"I'm ruined. I've been smoking reefers for years. I knew I would get caught sooner or later. This is the bitter end."

Film star Robert Mitchum (opposite) on his arrest for marijuana possession in 1948. He was sentenced to 60 days in prison. His next film, the family favorite, The Red Pony, *was made immediately after his release.*

cannabis-based drugs. Americans were going through a kind of general drug withdrawal. The public was just waking up to the addictive effects of the drugs found in hundreds of patent medicines, potions, and products, including Coke, which contained cocaine.

From the earliest days, marijuana was associated with groups who made average, middle-class Americans nervous. The roots of cannabis' problems in the United States reach back to the 1870s, when people in the New World first started smoking the drug for fun.

An old man is surrounded by "demon rum" and "other monsters," including hashish, in this 1919 cartoon by Oliver Hereford.

53

La Cucarachas

Pancho Villa's revolutionary army got an extra shot of courage through regular use of marijuana. His exhausted soldiers, some of them pictured here in this 1914 photo, are immortalized in the folk song "La Cucaracha." The still familiar song tells the sad tale of one of Pancho's depleted "cockroaches," who has run out of marijuana to smoke. "Roach," a nickname for a marijuana cigarette butt, comes from *cucaracha*.

Marijuana use took off in early American border towns
such as El Paso (above) and New Orleans (opposite) in the early 1900s.

They were workers, virtual slaves, in the Caribbean, Brazil, and Central America, who took to toking to escape from the rigors of their backbreaking labor. Life in the sugarcane fields was tough, the days were long and hot; cannabis took their minds off their troubles with the added benefit of no hangover in the morning.

Around the same time, cannabis cigarettes were gaining favor in Mexico, and Pancho Villa's revolutionary army got an extra shot of courage through regular use of the drug. The word "marijuana," which some reports say is Mexican for "intoxicant," first came into use, while the drug itself began to weed its way into the popular imagination. The still familiar folk song "La Cucaracha" was making the rounds, and in its original Spanish told the story of one of Pancho's exhausted "cockroaches." This is the origin of the word "roach," a nickname for a marijuana cigarette butt. The cockroaches or foot soldiers were in need of a little inspiration to help carry on the fight:

> *The cockroach, the cockroach,*
> *Now cannot walk,*
> *Because he don't, because he don't*
> *Have marijuana to smoke . . .*

By the turn of the century pot was popping up in American port and border towns. Brought by sailors, soldiers, and migrant workers — most of whom were Mexican or black — marijuana use was limited to isolated

Cannabis sativa *has been the primary material for ropemaking thoughout history. In 1860, the American output of hemp rope was some 74,000 tons, enough to lasso a nation and win the West. In the States, hemp was grown chiefly in the blue grass regions of Kentucky and Tennessee.*

pockets in America's Deep South, places such as El Paso, Texas, and the storied Storyville section of New Orleans. This latter connection gave a new face to marijuana in the U.S., that of the predominantly black jazz musician. Storyville was the birthplace of jazz, as well as home to New Orleans' urban poor population, so it's no surprise jazz cats were hip to the hemp. In fact, the drug undoubtedly had a hand in shaping the evolution of jazz music, just as psychedelics changed the shape of rock music in the 1960s; many musicians tried to capture in their solos the sense of wild freedom they felt under the influence of marijuana. Still, pot use was sporadic; in time, the drug moved north up the Mississippi River, through the Ohio Valley, then east to New York City, but pot never ignited the popular imagination; few people really cared about drugs. White, middle-class Americans, who made up the majority of voters, associated marijuana with Mexicans, blacks, and the poor, and by extension, with crime and other immoral behavior. Racist temperaments were probably in play when New Orleans banned the drug in 1923. A couple of years later, Louisiana joined the ban, and by the end of the Prohibition era, seventeen states had cannabis bans on the books.

Of course, the American people were already in a sour mood. In 1920, the Eighteenth Amendment was passed into law and the era of Prohibition had begun. The commercial manufacture and sale of alcohol was banned, although people could still make liquor at home for their personal use. It was

mythinformation

HEMP IMPOSTERS

Many plants claim to produce hemp. *Cannabis sativa*, however, is the only one to produce true hemp. Manila hemp and sisal hemp, the most common impersonators, are misnomers. Manila hemp, or *abaca*, is grown in the Philippines, and is important for cordage. It is of the same genus as the common banana, which it closely resembles except its fruit is inedible. Cultivated since the 16th century, Manila hemp has strong and durable fibers just like *Cannabis sativa*. Sisal hemp's botanical name is *agave*, and is also used for cordage. The basic difference: true hemp fiber from *Cannabis sativa* is extracted from the stems, whereas the fibers for *abaca* and sisal are located in the leaves.

a victory for the American temperance movement, which saw alcohol as the scourge of the nation, and for big business, which was well aware of the negative relationship between liquor and productivity. But neither of these groups predicted the consequences of Prohibition. Overnight, the booze business moved underground into the speakeasies and private clubs, and once liquor became scarce, other drugs gained favor.

While the U.S. was getting a sobering lesson on the pitfalls of alcohol control, the rest of the world was experimenting in a little prohibition of its own. In 1911, South Africa became the first League of Nation country to ban

"Musicians. And I'm not speaking about good musicians, but the jazz type."

The quote that brought an onslaught of public reaction against drug enforcer Harry Anslinger when replying to the Senate Committee in 1948 about who was using marijuana.

cannabis. It was a business move, pure and simple. Indian workers, brought in to work the mines, had introduced cannabis to South Africa some twenty years earlier, and the government soon figured out that pot undermined the mine workers' productivity. South Africa pushed for other countries to adopt their pot prohibition at The Hague Conference or first "Opium Conference" in 1912. Governments agreed to limit the manufacture and sale of opium, heroine, and cocaine. Although cannabis was mentioned in passing, opium was considered the big menace at the time, and little attention was paid to regulating pot.

Many people believe that Harry Anslinger (opposite) was single-handedly responsible for branding a little-known plant — cannabis — as public enemy number one.

However, in 1924, a delegation of European, African, and Middle Eastern countries signed the Geneva International Convention on Narcotic Control, banning the non-medical use of opiates, cocaine, and cannabis. This last drug barely made the list; it was added at the insistence of Egypt and Turkey, where abuse of the most potent form of cannabis — hashish — ran rampant. India hotly opposed this late addition; a *bhang* ban would be impossible to enforce, the Indians complained. For their part, the British delegation didn't care either way. There was very little recreational use of the drug in the U.K. and no public outcry against it. As long as tea wasn't on the list, the Brits couldn't care one way or the other. In the end, Britain abstained from the

vote on cannabis, but signed the treaty anyway. They continued to drag their heels, though, and didn't get around to passing their domestic Dangerous Drugs Act until 1928. And thus the legal use of *bhang* ended in many countries, not with a bang, but with a whimper.

Back in the U.S., public support for Prohibition was drying up. Americans liked their liquor and few were prepared for the crime wave the Eighteenth Amendment had set in motion. In 1933, Prohibition was repealed. During the dry decade, cannabis use had increased somewhat, but with Americans bellying up to the bar again, pot seemed destined to slip into obscurity. And it might have if it hadn't been for the efforts of a young bureaucrat trying to make a name for himself. Harry

Jazz musicians such as Louis Armstrong (below), who was arrested for pot possession in 1930, and Fats Waller (opposite) were targeted by Anslinger and his henchmen.

"At first you was a misdemeanor. But as the years rolled by you lost your 'misde' and got meaner and meaner." *Louis Armstrong on the criminalization of marijuana. From* Louis *by Max Jones and John Chilton.*

Anslinger first made waves during Prohibition, fighting rum runners out of the American Consulate in the West Indies. By 1930, he'd been put in charge of a brand new government agency, the Federal Bureau of Narcotics. Among his many talents, Anslinger was a master of public relations, and set out to prove himself worthy of his new job by initiating a personal vendetta against a little-known drug: cannabis.

The ladies meet for "tea" in this 1876 drawing from The Illustrated Police News.

"Marijuana inflames the erotic impulses and leads to revolting sex crimes."

London's Daily Mirror, *1924.*

MARIJUANA joints

Tea pads were all the rage in the 1930s.

YOU CAN CALL it "boo," "grass," "pot," "muggles." Marijuana has many nicknames including "tea." Some people even suspect the innocuous-sounding Tin Pan Alley song "Tea for Two" isn't really about the refreshing drink. In the early '30s, "tea pads" proliferated in New York City, especially in Harlem. Not to be confused with opium dens, but not unlike them either, tea pads were a place to go to socialize with other marijuana aficionados. They were rooms or apartments, even pup tents set up on the roofs of buildings, where you could go to buy and smoke pot. There is even evidence that tea pads existed a lot earlier and in more upscale neighborhoods, as the drawing opposite shows. It appeared in *The Illustrated Police News* in 1876 with the caption "Secret Dissipation of New York Belles: Interior of a Hasheesh Hell on Fifth Avenue."

In "Tea for a Viper," a 1938 article in *The New Yorker*, reporter Meyer Berger describes his first experience with a tea pad. "The only illumination in Chappy's place was a blue bulb glowing in the glass case of the slot-machine phonograph. All tea pads, or marijuana joints, use the blue lamps and nickel machines to induce and sustain the hashish mood. They play special recordings of viper, or weed, songs with weird ritualistic themes." Tea pads were so

underground that even a savvy reporter like Berger, familiar with New York's underbelly, took weeks to get into one. People would come and go. Some would just buy their weed and go, others would stay and get high. Berger showed his unhip "I was not a viper" side when he misquoted the words to "If You're a Viper" in the article. Instead of "Dreamed about a reefer five feet long/Mighty Mezz but not too strong," Berger misquoted the line, "Mighty immense, but not too strong." Apparently Berger wasn't familiar with Milton "Mezz" Mezzrow, a white Jewish kid who hung out in Harlem. Mezz, a sometime jazz musician, is best known for the great grass he supplied.

In 1944, *The LaGuardia Report*, commissioned by New York Mayor Fiorello LaGuardia to investigate the city's alleged drug problem, described tea pads: "The marihuana smoker derives greater satisfaction if he is smoking in the presence of others. His attitude in the 'tea-pad' is that of a relaxed individual, free from the anxieties and cares of the realities of life. The 'tea-pad' takes on the atmosphere of a very congenial social club.... A constant observation was the extreme willingness to share and puff on each other's cigarettes." Tea pads may not be around anymore, but some things never change.

Realizing that the pen was mightier than the sword, Anslinger began planting sensational anti-cannabis stories, many of them self-penned, in magazines and newspapers across the nation. From the darkest recesses of Anslinger's mind came articles with titles like "Marihuana: Assassin of Youth," which told tales of dope-dazed farmers who raped their daughters and cannabis-crazed college kids ax-murdering friends and families. Often the tales had decidedly racist undertones, as the criminals were, more often than not, black or Hispanic, and without question brought the term "marijuana" to mainstream America for the first time. These lurid tales were gleefully reprinted in America's newspapers. This has led some contemporary commentators to wonder if some of the press were in cahoots with Anslinger in an effort to undermine the legitimate hemp fiber industry. However, the collapse of the American hemp industry probably had more to do with a host of different reasons, including the new cheap tropical fibers that were on the scene, a lack of processing machinery and funding during the depression, not to mention a drought in the Midwest.

"Dreamed about a reefer five feet long / Mighty Mezz but not too strong."

From the song "If You're a Viper," by Stuff Smith, recorded by Fats Waller in the '40s about Milton Mezzrow, known to score superior weed.

In any case, Anslinger's smokescreen worked. There was a public outcry against this dreaded drug, prompting Anslinger to propose the Marihuana Tax Act, a law restricting cannabis use. The proposed law moved forward with little public interest; only the American Medical Association raised a voice of dissent. The doctors expressed surprise when they were told that "marijuana" in fact referred to good old American hemp. Dr. William C. Woodward, the AMA's spokesman at the Congressional Hemp Hearings, criticized the lack of scientific evidence behind the bill, and the vague wording which colored its every detail. More to the point, he said that doctors did not consider marijuana a health risk and, indeed, believed there was value in exploring the healing potential of the drug. But the doctors' protests went unnoticed, literally. During the brief debate in the House of Representatives, the Speaker wrongly asserted that the AMA supported it.

mythinformation

A RECIPE IS A RECIPE IS A RECIPE

Alice B. Toklas, confidante and lover of Gertrude Stein,
was not the hashish queen history has made her out to be.

ALICE B. TOKLAS loved to cook. This is undisputed. But the recipe for Hashisch Fudge that appeared in *The Alice B. Toklas Cookbook* was not hers. Furthermore, she was shocked when she realized what the recipe contained. The story starts in the early 1950s after the death of Gertrude Stein, when Toklas is approached to

Alice Babette Toklas (below right) and Gertrude Stein arrive in New York in 1934.

write a cookbook. She decided to have a chapter of recipes contributed by friends. One of the friends, Brion Gysin, also a friend of Paul and Jane Bowles, and a visitor to Morocco, contributed Hashisch Fudge. The introduction which mentions the recipe would be perfect for a ladies' bridge club or how in Morocco it was good for warding off the common cold is also his. Clearly, Toklas didn't test the recipe and the odd spelling of cannabis as "canibus" threw her off and she innocently included the recipe in the book. In *Staying on Alone: Letters of Alice B. Toklas*, edited by Edward Burns, she wrote to a friend how shocked she was by a review in *Time* that commented on the recipe: "I was also furious until I discovered it was really in the cookbook!" Friend Thornton Wilder said no one would believe in her innocence and that she had pulled off the best publicity stunt of the year. Although the recipe did appear in the British publication of the book, it was edited out of the American version.

Here's how myths get started: maybe toking came from Toklas!

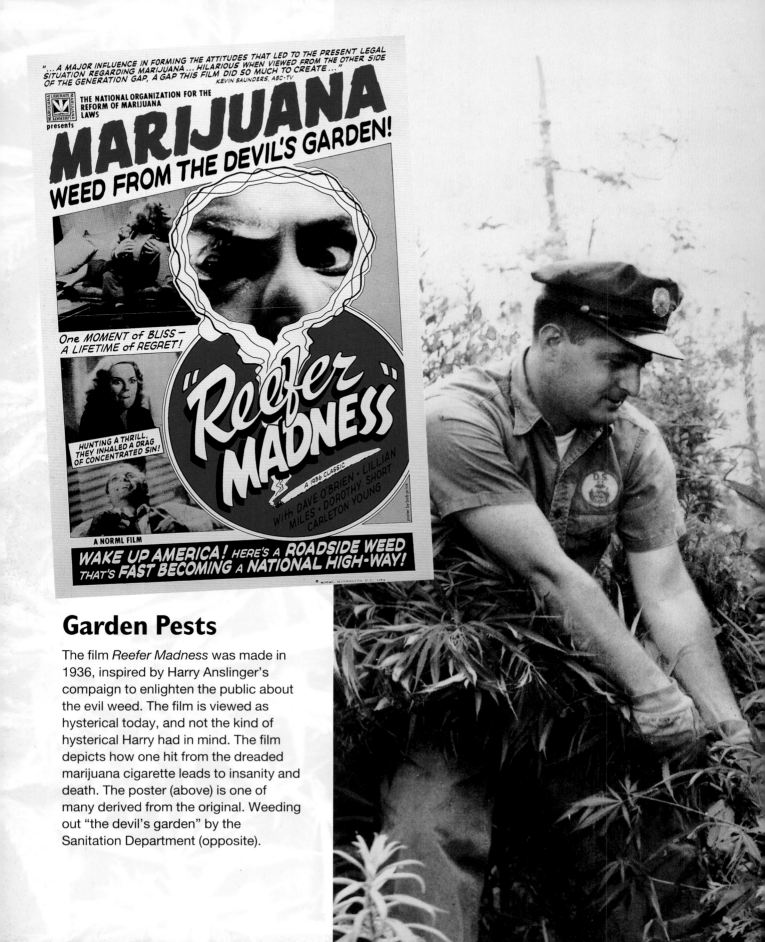

THE NATIONAL ORGANIZATION FOR THE REFORM OF MARIJUANA LAWS
presents

MARIJUANA
WEED FROM THE DEVIL'S GARDEN!

One MOMENT of BLISS — A LIFETIME of REGRET!

HUNTING A THRILL, THEY INHALED A DRAG OF CONCENTRATED SIN!

"Reefer" MADNESS

A 1936 CLASSIC

With DAVE O'BRIEN · LILLIAN MILES · DOROTHY SHORT CARLETON YOUNG

poster by bob price

A NORML FILM

WAKE UP AMERICA! HERE'S A ROADSIDE WEED THAT'S FAST BECOMING A NATIONAL HIGH-WAY!

© NORML WASHINGTON, D.C. 1974

Garden Pests

The film *Reefer Madness* was made in 1936, inspired by Harry Anslinger's compaign to enlighten the public about the evil weed. The film is viewed as hysterical today, and not the kind of hysterical Harry had in mind. The film depicts how one hit from the dreaded marijuana cigarette leads to insanity and death. The poster (above) is one of many derived from the original. Weeding out "the devil's garden" by the Sanitation Department (opposite).

In fact, Speaker Sam Rayburn seemed to know nothing about the Marihuana Tax Act he was encouraging the House to accept. When asked about the purpose of the proposed law, Rayburn shrugged. "I don't know," he said. "It has something to do with a thing called marijuana." And so the act passed into law on October 1, 1937. It placed restrictive taxes on cannabis, effectively prohibiting its use. Anyone using the drug for industrial or medical purposes had to pay one dollar per ounce to the government coffers; anyone using it for recreational purposes was subject to a $100-an-ounce tax. People who failed to comply with the new tax were subject to fines or prison terms. One week later, a certain Samuel Caldwell of Colorado earned the dubious distinction of being the first person tried under the new rules. Charged with selling a small amount of grass, he earned four years hard labor at the notorious Leavenworth Prison.

Still, cannabis had its supporters. No less than Henry Ford was experimenting with soybean-based plastics, and in 1937 introduced a prototype automobile, made from soybeans and other organic components, including a plastic reinforced with hemp. (Somehow, though, it never made it into production.) And during World War II, the government conveniently forgot all its previous concern and encouraged farmers to "Grow Hemp for Victory." Cut off by the Japanese from the established Asian hemp supply, America needed a reliable source of fiber for everything from rope to the soldiers' shoelaces. Farmers in the Midwest planted some 300,000 acres of cannabis, but the program was abandoned when the war ended, leaving vast meadows of marijuana growing wild. You can still find it today as "ditch weed," a very low potency marijuana, which offers its users a hyperventilation high and a four-alarm headache.

Once Anslinger landed marijuana in the public's bad books, he used his best efforts to keep it there. He turned his attention to the world of jazz music, where he believed, quite accurately, that marijuana laws were being widely ignored. He ordered Federal Bureau of Narcotic operatives to go undercover and keep tabs on virtually every jazz and swing musician of the era, everyone from Louis Armstrong, Duke Ellington, Mezz Mezzrow, Cab Calloway, and Jimmy Dorsey to members of the NBC Orchestra and Milton Berle's house band. But Anslinger failed as a music critic. In 1948, he went

Henry Ford takes a whack at the rear deck of the first organic car to prove its durability. The whole-earth car, developed in the '40s, had a plastic body made from several common crops including soybeans, hemp, and other raw materials.

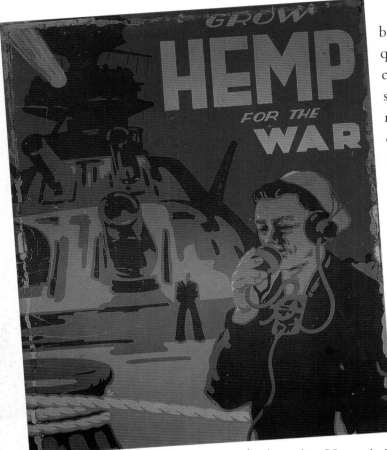

Poster encouraging farmers to grow hemp during World War II (above). Inspecting hemp grown for seed (opposite). Shocks of hemp (overleaf).

before a Senate committee, requesting more agents for his anti-cannabis campaign. When asked specifically who was breaking the marijuana laws, Anslinger declared, "Musicians. And I'm not speaking about good musicians, but the jazz type." This slight of an American entertainment institution did not go unnoticed. Anslinger was denounced in newspapers across the country, and a flood of angry letters flowed into his office at the Treasury Department.

Today, marijuana advocates look back in anger at Anslinger, painting him as the man who single-handedly destroyed the hemp industry in America. He probably wouldn't dispute the charge, either; he was a proud campaigner against pot. What's forgotten, though, is that his campaign to rid the country of the marijuana menace went on largely unopposed. By the end of the 1940s, few people cared about cannabis; farmers weren't growing it, there just wasn't the demand, while the country's craftspeople and artisans were experimenting with exciting new fibers. It was a time when synthetic fibers ruled, when nylon was in greater demand than silk, and the whole world waited to embrace the next wonder of modern technology. Cannabis, this relic from the Stone Ages, had little place in the Age of Plastic. But thanks in large part to Anslinger's bad press, marijuana had caught the attention of the public, piquing the curiosity of an entire generation, and paving the way for the coming cannabis craze.

72

IT AIN'T HAY

DAVID DODGE

WITH CRIME MAP ON BACK COVER

A DELL THRILLER

PULP fiction

No doubt inspired by Harry Anslinger's rants and raves about the "evil" marijuana, anti-dope books were very popular in the '40s and '50s. The covers, usually depicting big-breasted women hanging out in unsavory locales, were often more powerful than the stories inside. The plot lines were as inauthentic as the characters, which often featured gun-totting, marijuana-addicted losers. All the paperbacks featured here were written well after *The LaGuardia Report* concluded that marijuana wasn't any more harmful to society than alcohol — evidence that cultural attitudes, and not empirical studies, have often influenced cannabis prohibition.

IT AIN'T HAY

A Dell thriller by David Dodge, cover art by Gerald Gregg, first published by Simon and Schuster in 1946. Back cover line: "Where marijuana and murder make a thrilling story." Hay, another nickname for marijuana, features in this book about dope smuggling. Favorite quote: "Marijuana doesn't do anything to the inner man except undress him."

MUSK, HASHISH AND BLOOD

An Avon book by Hector France, cover artist unknown, first published in the '20s. This edition 1951. Front cover line: "The adventures of a modern man among the cruel men and passionate women of Algiers." Enough said.

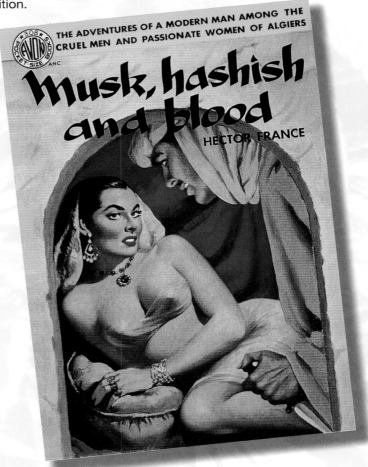

77

MARIHUANA
A Dell book by William Irish, cover art by Bill Fleming. This edition 1951.
The most famous of the anti-dope genre, this book features Mr. King Turner, who gets stoned and goes on a killing rampage. Cornell Hopley Woolrich (aka William Irish) was a well-known crime novelist whose work includes *Night Has a Thousand Eyes* and *The Bride Wore Black*. The striking cover is often copied and remains a valuable collectible today.

DOPE, INC.
An Avon book by Joachim Joesten, cover art by Owen Kampen. Published in 1953. This is a non-fiction book supposedly telling you the "facts" about marijuana. However, with phrases that include "hashish-crazed Orientals," "invariably leads to epilepsy and insanity," and "medical uses are extremely slight and often non-existent," the book reads more like bad fiction.

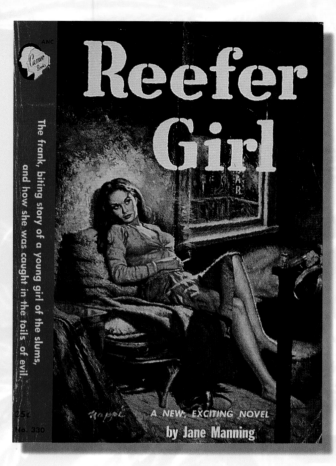

REEFER GIRL
A Cameo Book by Jane Manning, cover art by Rudolph Nappi. Published in 1953.

REEFER BOY
Pedigree Books by Hal Ellson, cover artist unknown. This edition 1957.

Both *Reefer Girl*, which is an American Book, and *Reefer Boy*, a British publication, play to parents' fears and worst nightmares about pot. Either your daughter will end up stoned and abandoned in a cheap room, or your son will fall in with the wrong crowd and become a teenage dope addict.

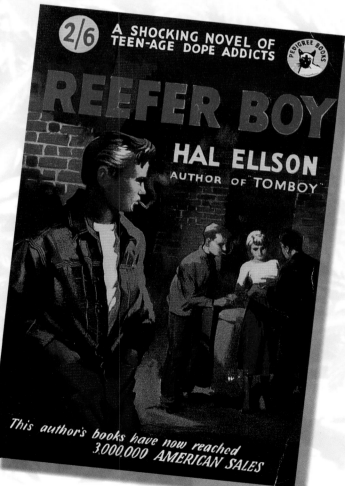

CHAPTER FIVE

Everybody Must Get Stoned

FROM THE BEATS IN THE '50s TO THE HIPPIES IN THE '60s

AS ANSLINGER'S STAR descended, marijuana's warm glow grew stronger. The drug first showed signs of life in 1944, when the prestigious New York Academy of Medicine issued the results of a long-term marijuana study. The report concluded there was no evidence the recreational use of marijuana

"With my inexhaustible supply of Elitch, I daily dive into these dim regions and crawl to the surface with the stub of a pencil, sweating, to record what I have observed." *Jack Kerouac, commenting on a summer he spent in Denver, refers to marijuana as "Elitch," after the amusement park where he and his pals gathered to get stoned.*

caused people to become violent, or insane, or raving drug addicts. Predictably, Anslinger went nuts. He called the authors of the study "dangerous" and stepped up his anti-marijuana campaign to counteract the report. But the seeds had been planted, and many Americans wanted to know the real dope on pot.

The 1950s saw a boom in pot's popularity around the globe. In 1951, the United Nations released its *Bulletin of Narcotic Drugs* which stated that there were more than 200 million cannabis users worldwide. A report in the magazine *Newsweek* claimed that 100,000 Americans had used pot, although the drug had little impact outside of jazz clubs and the homes of the urban poor. Likewise in England, marijuana was largely restricted to musicians and West Indian immigrants, yet even a well-organized, and much-publicized, police sweep of London jazz clubs in the early fifties resulted in few arrests: they found more doobie doobie wawa's than doobies. That didn't stop the British government from stepping up its fight against cannabis, and in 1955 it followed America's example and banned hemp farming.

Bob Hope (below left) and James Garner imitate beatniks on an episode of "The Bob Hope Buick Show" in 1959.

Jack Kerouac (left) holding William Burroughs' cat outside the Villa Mouneria, Tangier, in 1957. Kerouac rented a spacious upstairs floor with veranda for $40 a month.

The United States was taking the lead in pressing other countries to prohibit pot, but as the 1950s progressed, a shift in marijuana habits was under way. There was a new generation of liberal-minded middle-class whites, raised on jazz, looking to redefine their world. It was the folk music boom, when any kid with a guitar could become a musician — and in the process get a sniff of the music business underworld, where marijuana use abounded. Meanwhile, Beat Generation writers like Jack Kerouac, William S. Burroughs, and Allen Ginsberg inspired young people to find new ways of expressing themselves.

Kerouac, in particular, was one of the original addict writers, who spent his time in a hobolike existence drifting throughout the States. He apparently smoked his first joint while listening to jazz in Harlem. Eventually he worked

"TEA" TIME AT *THE TIMES* British jazz singer and critic George Melly (opposite) was an early champion of the decriminalization of marijuana. Although he preferred alcohol over "tea" himself, he didn't hesitate to sign the famous ad in *The Times* in 1967, placed by SOMA — a group named after the rapturous narcotic of Aldous Huxley's *Brave New World* — denouncing England's marijuana laws as "immoral in principle and unworkable in practice." The letter was signed by more than 60 public figures, including Jonathan Aitken, a future politician, and all four members of the Beatles. In the wake of the pro-pot protests, the British government tabled *The Wootton Report*, a review of current drug policies that recommended the legalization of pot possession.

his way to Mexico City where he smoked powerful grass, and tried to write. In 1957, *On the Road* was published. It featured a hero not unlike Kerouac who rejected the establishment. Some say it marked the beginning of the modern drug culture. Marijuana was just one of the many drugs that Kerouac embraced; he used mescaline and peyote, and was introduced to morphine and heroine by Burroughs. But the main intoxicant throughout his career was alcohol, and it was that drug that eventually killed him when he was forty-seven.

The sands of society were beginning to shift, and predictably the old guards were growing nervous. It was the Cold War era where, faced with massive social change and a real enemy from without, America began to root out Communist sympathizers. The witch hunt soon spread to include anyone whose behavior pierced the narrowly defined social norms. In light of the rise in marijuana use, particularly among young men, many came to see the drug as a symptom, if not cause, of the moral decay of the age.

Did they or didn't they?

In the 1946 film *A Night in Casablanca*, the Marx Brothers were more likely to be seen running around with tilted fezzes on their heads than smoking hookahs as this publicity shot for the film shows. It's not clear if the brothers actually partook in cannabis, but in the documentary *The Unknown Marx Brothers* (Crew Neck Productions), Chico explains that Groucho got his nickname by wearing what was known as a "grouch bag" around his neck. Chico joked, "In this bag we would keep our pennies, our marbles, a piece of candy, a little marijuana, whatever we could pick up." As the audience laughs, Chico adds, "Well, we were studying to be musicians."

m y t h i n f o r m a t i o n

HEMPLESS JEANS

No, Levi's® jeans were never ever made from hemp. Levi Strauss & Co. is very adamant on this point. It seems the confusion arose from a pair of jeans made in the late 1800s from brown duck fabric, which looked like canvas, but was, in fact, cotton. Somehow, someone jumped to the conclusion that canvas, which can sometimes be made from cannabis, meant the jeans were made from hemp. They weren't. They aren't. And, it appears, they never will be.

In 1951, New York State Senator Everett Dirksen proposed that criminals convicted of marijuana and other drug offenses get the death penalty, while his colleague Congressman Edwin Arthur Hall, a more forgiving sort, suggested that a mandatory 100-year jail term would suffice. Later that year, the Senate investigated the growing drug menace and singled out marijuana as the key "gateway" or stepping-stone drug, which tempted unsuspecting people into hard-core addiction. From the start, the scientific community questioned this theory; just because some addicts started off on marijuana suggested nothing about the causes of addiction. The gateway theory also fails to explain why most people who try marijuana hardly ever become addicted to it — in fact, physical addiction to marijuana is rare, although some people develop a psychological dependence on it — or any other drug.

The theory did the job. In the fall of 1951, Congress passed the Boggs Act, which called for two- to-five-year mandatory minimum sentences for even first-time drug offenders. Pot users were penalized at the same level as heroin. The new law raised the hackles, and probably shackles, of no less than James Bennett, the man in charge of U.S. prisons. Bennett called the law "hysterical." He urged judges to oppose it. They did, and called on the federal government to remove the mandatory minimum sentence clause. Instead, lawmakers upped the ante, increasing jail terms in a revised Narcotics Control Act, passed in 1956.

The details of the drug laws are well documented, but no one has yet explained why the senators went out of their way to attack marijuana users.

Besides marijuana, these two college students had something to read on them when they were arrested for narcotics possession in the mid '60s. One of the books, by Aldous Huxley who is best known for his seminal novel about drugs, Brave New World, *seems a fitting choice here.*

Maybe politicians had caught a whiff of the burgeoning civil rights movement and were getting all hot and bothered. Since in the popular mind marijuana users were either black or Hispanic, these tough marijuana laws were one more way to keep minorities in line. It's perhaps telling that the toughest anti-marijuana laws were found in southern states like Louisiana, where simple possession could net you ninety-nine years in the state pen, and Georgia, where the rule of thumb was two strikes, you're out, way out, in fact, dead. That's right. Anyone convicted of selling marijuana to a minor twice could be given the death penalty.

The 1960s saw a dramatic shift in the public's perception of pot. At first,

"Now these things aren't drugs; they just bend your mind a little. I think everybody's mind should be bent once in a while."

Bob Dylan in a 1966 Playboy *interview.*

Bob Dylan (opposite) gets high at the George V Hotel in Paris in 1966, the year his single "Rainy Day Women #12 & 35" was banned from radio for its refrain "Everybody must get stoned."

the U.S. continued to press its anti-pot policies on the rest of the world. In 1961, Harry Anslinger reemerged to lead the American contingent in a series of UN talks aimed at achieving a total worldwide ban on cannabis production and use by the year 1990. More than sixty countries signed the UN Single Convention on Narcotic Drugs, including Mexico, Canada and the United States. A year later Anslinger resigned, and President Kennedy — who was rumored to smoke pot to relieve chronic back pain — put together a committee to study the nation's narcotic problem. To a country used to anti-marijuana hysteria, the commission's final report was simply astonishing. It asserted that the hazards of marijuana "have been exaggerated" and that the harsh criminal penalties for recreational users were "in poor social perspective." Soon afterwards, lawmakers finally made a distinction between marijuana and other harsher drugs. What had happened? The generation that had grown up in the 1950s, through the first folk boom and advent of rock 'n' roll, were moving into the circles of power. Not only did they have a healthy suspicion of their elders, but many of them had firsthand experience with pot, and knew that it wasn't the menace it was cracked up to be.

As pot made the quantum leap from backstreets and jazz clubs to college campuses, it quickly became the drug of choice for a generation of young artists. The pop music world was particularly fond of pot. As rock icons came out in support of the drug, fans searched the songs of the Beatles, the Rolling Stones, and Bob Dylan — whose 1966 single "Rainy Day Women #12 & 35" was banned from radio for its refrain "Everybody must get stoned" — for subtle and not-so-subtle drug allusions. Why did weed take the pop world by storm? In part, it had something to do with marijuana's bad-boy image; one of the first lessons the rock industry learned is that rebellion sells records. In part, it was an age of experimentation, when the credo of the crowd was "Do your own thing."

Rolling Stones Keith Richard and Mick Jagger (opposite) are all smiles after their court appearance on drug charges in 1967. The Beatles (below) in 1965 were introduced to pot by Bob Dylan.

"We were smoking marijuana for breakfast." *John Lennon in 1965.*

Bob Dylan, the most influential American musician of the time, probably did as much to popularize pot as anyone. He was said to have caught the marijuana bug as a student in Minnesota, where the drug was in common use in his old haunt, the bohemian Dinkytown section of Minneapolis. Dylan admitted his fondness for pot to *Playboy* magazine in 1966; the year before, as the legend goes, he introduced the Beatles to the weed during their first American tour. The Fab Four quickly developed a taste for the drug — "We were smoking marijuana for breakfast," John Lennon later said. In 1966, British folksinger Donovan became the first well-known pop star arrested for pot possession; he got off with a $500 fine and a stern warning.

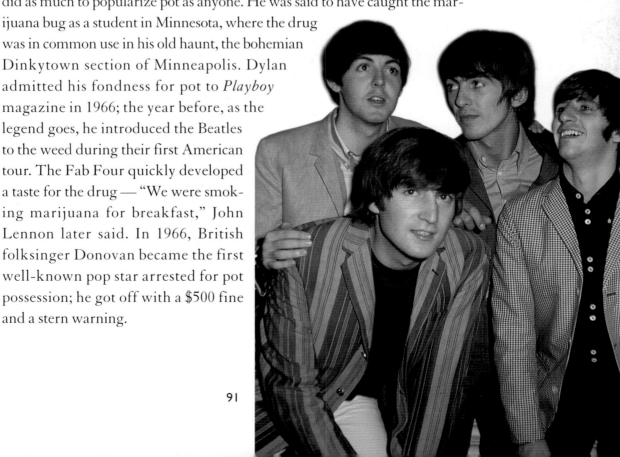

The Wasteland

No smoking gun here as a Vietnam soldier (opposite) takes a break. The Vietnam War introduced millions of young American soldiers to marijuana. Grass was freely available overseas, and as much as 75 percent of the soldiers stationed in Vietnam smoked pot at some point.

"Much of the prevailing public apprehension about marijuana may stem from the drug's effect of inducing introspection and bodily passivity, which are antipathetic to a culture that values aggressiveness, achievement, and activity."

Excerpt from definition of marijuana, The New Columbia Encyclopedia, *edited by William H. Harris and Judith S. Levey, 1975.*

A year later, the rock world was rocked when Rolling Stone Keith Richard was arrested on marijuana charges. Police had raided his house, Redlands, in southern England, during a wild party and found, among other things, a nude woman under a bearskin rug. The police said Richard and his guests were high on pot, a charge they denied; the supposedly stoned Stone was sentenced to one year in prison and a $1,000 fine. This launched a public outcry against the police, and even the conservative London *Times* came to Richard's defense, saying the punishment was far too severe. Eventually, the

"The actual experience of the smoked herb has been clouded by a fog of dirty language perpetrated by a crowd of fakers who have not had the experience and yet insist on downgrading it."

Allen Ginsberg from "The Great Marijuana Hoax," a 1966 article in The Atlantic Monthly.

Poet Allen Ginsberg (opposite) leads a group of demonstrators in 1965 demanding the release of prisoners busted for marijuana.

case went to appeal, where it was overturned on a minor technicality: the police hadn't found any pot on the premises. The resulting publicity galvanized the pro-pot movement in England. A few months after Richard's ordeal, a group calling itself SOMA — named after the rapturous narcotic of Aldous Huxley's *Brave New World* — published an open letter in *The Times* denouncing England's marijuana laws as "immoral in principle and unworkable in practice." The letter was signed by more than sixty public figures, including Jonathan Aitken, a future politician, and all four members of the Beatles. Soon afterwards, more than three thousand showed up for a SOMA "smoke-in" in London's Hyde Park. In the wake of the pro-pot protests, the British government tabled *The Wootton Report*, a review of current drug policies that recommended the legalization of pot possession. Britain, it seemed, was leading the Western world into a whole new way of thinking about the weed.

Although the pop world embraced pot, few people outside that realm had actually tried the stuff. It was still hard to obtain and relatively expensive, compared to booze. What really got things rolling was the Vietnam War, which introduced millions of young Americans to the drug. Marijuana

Life magazine's 1969 cover story on marijuana reported that 12 million Americans had tried pot. Thirty years later that number is now more than 70 million. A test subject (opposite) from the Life article puffs for science as a research psychiatrist from the University of California applies electrodes to his head to monitor brain responses while the earphones record sensitivity to sound.

was freely available overseas, and as much as seventy-five percent of the soldiers stationed in Vietnam smoked pot at some point.

Meanwhile, marijuana was finally breaking through to the masses. The year was 1967, the Summer of Love, and marijuana set the mood. The hip hippie icebreaker, marijuana was the martini of its day. But it also served an important social function, a symbol that galvanized the antiwar counterculture. And so cannabis had come full circle, from marijuana menace to Love Drug, bolstering the hopes and aspirations of a generation. Like rock 'n' roll, marijuana was here to stay, and despite the best efforts of the pot party poopers, its popularity continued to grow.

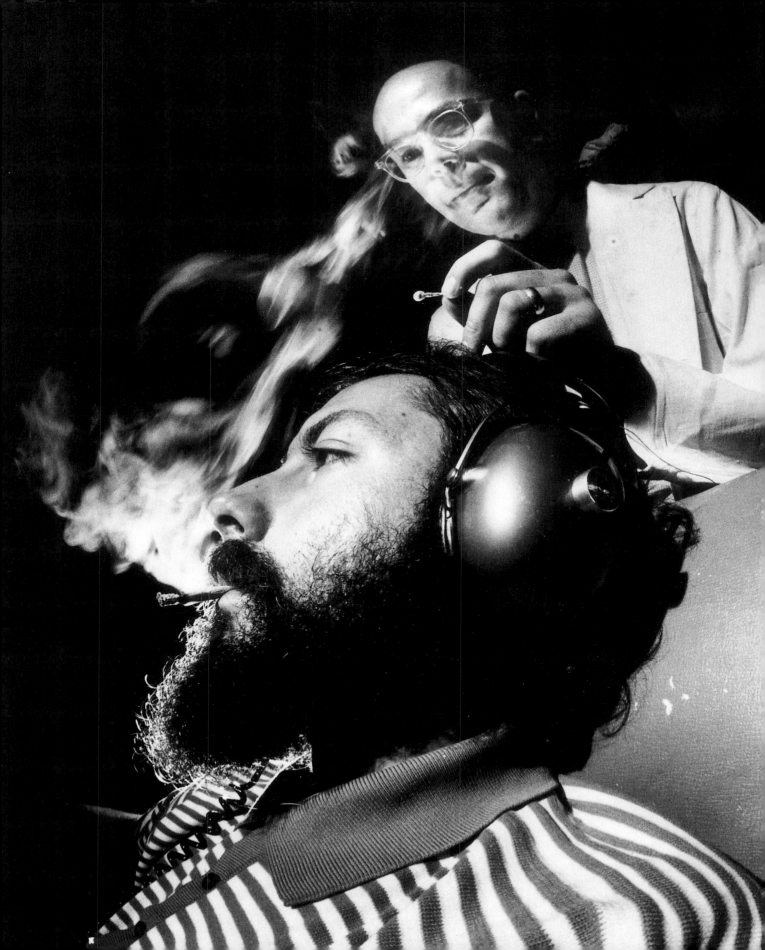

HIGHWAY to heaven

The counterculture travels the Hippie Trail to the Far East
in search of spiritualism and drugs.

PAUL BOWLES, GERTRUDE STEIN, and William Burroughs had already traveled there in the '40s and '50s. The invisible thread linking one generation to the next continued when the hippies in the '60s and '70s made their way to Tangier, one of the first stops on what came to be known as the Hippie Trail. They came from Europe and North America in droves, escaping the suburbs, searching for enlightenment and hashish. From Morocco, they then journeyed to Istanbul, one of the major markets for hashish, through Iran to Afghanistan, eventually finding their way to Goa and Katmandu.

There were few laws then governing the use and sale of hashish, which was openly sold in coffee shops and bazaars, often in colorful shapes and coils. In Katmandu alone, there were more than 30 hashish shops that became

What was supposed to be a brief vacation turned into a lifelong stay for writer Paul Bowles (below) when he visited Morocco on the advice of Gertrude Stein. Hippies (opposite) in Tangier partake of the local delicacy kif, *the Moroccan name for marijuana.*

LET US TAKE HIGHER
Phone : 13863

EDEN HASHISH CENTRE

Oldest & Favourite Shop in Town Serving you the Best Nepalese Hash & Ganja
(Available Wholesale & Retail)
COME VISIT US ANY TIME FOR ALL YOUR HASHISH NEEDS

EDEN HASHISH CENTRE

OLD 5/1, Bashantpur, KATHMANDU
NEW 5/259, Ombahal, NEPAL
Prop. D. D. SHARMA

favorite hangouts for the counterculture. One of the more famous ones was the Eden Hashish Centre (see opposite and left.)

The great numbers of hippies traveling through these regions couldn't help but have a cultural impact on the hashish world. Such a huge demand was created that it caused changes in hashish production, including export and consumption, eventually leading to restrictions. Robert Connell Clarke describes the last carefree days in *Hashish!*: "The influx of counterculture travelers to Nepal in search of hashish instigated increased areas of cannabis cultivation, greatly inflated prices, and initiated large-scale smuggling from Nepal into India and abroad. It was estimated that by 1973 more hashish was exported than consumed within Nepal. Pressure from the United Nations and the United States to control cannabis production caused the Nepali government to begin closing the hashish shops in 1972. On July 16, 1973, all hashish dealers' licenses were revoked and the hashish shops were closed."

Nuggets of Nepalese hashish.

CHAPTER SIX

High and Mighty

WEED CONTROL IN THE '70s AND '80s

THE CANNABIS CRAZE of the sixties seemed to signal a new era. Ordinary people took a second look at the rules prohibiting marijuana. By 1970, the social use of the weed was widespread, and police across the Western world

"Yes, Rasta! Herb is the healing of the nation."   *Bob Marley in the early '70s.*

were overwhelmed by the sudden appearance of millions of casual pot smokers mainly from middle-class families.

In 1970, America's old Marihuana Tax Act — the "Anslinger" Act — was declared unconstitutional. That same year Keith Stroup founded a new pro-marijuana lobby group called the National Organization for the Reform of Marijuana Laws, or NORML for short. The Canadian government also warmed to the weed. In 1972, the federally appointed Le Dain Commission issued its final report, which recommended Canada seriously consider decriminalizing marijuana for personal use. Even Richard Nixon was getting into the act. Better known for break-ins than love-ins, Nixon publicly declared that he was against legalized marijuana. At the same time, he appointed the Shafer Commission to study the issue. However, in 1973, when the commission issued its report, it recommended that people should be allowed to possess pot for personal purposes, and that selling or giving away small amounts of the weed was nobody's business. For the first time, the American government recognized marijuana as a soft drug, in a league below cocaine and heroin. To no one's surprise, Congress scrapped most of the Boggs Act. Gone were

Bob Marley (opposite) and other Rastas considered marijuana a healing herb and sang its praises often. Album cover for 1970s Peter Tosh album (above) with his popular song about grass, "Legalize It," which was banned in Jamaica.

103

mandatory minimum sentences and the hard-nosed approach to drug use, earning praise from both parties, including words of support from a certain congressman, George Bush, who believed that the legal reforms would lead to "better justice and more appropriate sentences."

Things weren't going as smoothly in the rest of the Western world. Although lots of people smoked pot, there were very few changes in the

"They never spent a night apart, except for the 10 days McCartney spent in a Tokyo jail after he was arrested for marijuana possession."

New York Times *Obituary of Lady Linda McCartney, April 20, 1998, referring to Paul McCartney's arrest (opposite) in 1980*

A marijuana plant is displayed at Amsterdam's Cannabis College, a public education center that offers information on all uses of cannabis.

political climate. In France and Germany there was little serious talk of decriminalizing marijuana, although a growing informed sector of the public was campaigning for its reform. And in England the government started backpedaling. Ignoring *The Wootton Report* of the late 1960s, the government tabled the British Misuse of Drugs Act, which classified cannabis as a Class B drug, subject to stiff fines and jail sentences, and outlawing the medical use of cannabis. Holland led the cannabis charge in Europe. In 1972, that country's Baan Commission recommended that anyone caught with a quarter kilo or less of cannabis be charged with a misdemeanor only. Four years later, the country famous for windmills and wooden shoes introduced a new Dutch treat. The government stopped prosecuting petty pot offenders, and allowed some outlets — youth centers and coffee shops — to sell pot. In accordance with international agreement, pot was technically still illegal. But the Dutch government issued guidelines which prevented police from arresting anyone caught with thirty grams of marijuana or less.

Back in the States, in 1976, President Gerald Ford set up a special commission to look at the drug problem. This group concluded that marijuana did not pose any imminent threat to the health and well-being

of Americans, and that federal money would be best spent trying to bust up illegal drug cartels and manufacturers than hounding homegrown heads. If it sounded too good to be true, it was. Ford forgot to mention that part of his plan included air assaults on Mexican marijuana fields. In those days, most pot came from Mexico or Jamaica. Ford's idea was to spray the plants with a powerful herbicide called paraquat, once used to defoliate the jungles of

The wild and wacky stoners Cheech and Chong were known to include a giant rolling paper in their records. Another one of their albums, "Los Cochinos," (above) features a carload of grass.

Vietnam. It was bad news for Mexico's pot farmers, but it had an even worse effect on unsuspecting Americans who'd managed to get their hands on some of the tainted weed. It seems that paraquat left a poisonous residue on the plants, which, if eaten or inhaled, could cause respiratory problems, convulsions, kidney damage — even death.

For people who liked to get high, the Great Paraquat Scare of 1976 was the low point of the decade. Still, popular acceptance of pot was high — by the mid-seventies, forty million Americans had tried it. Forty years after the federal government introduced legislation to outlaw hemp, President Jimmy Carter slammed existing marijuana policy. "Penalties against possession of a drug should not be more damaging to an individual than the use of the drug itself," Carter said in a speech to Congress. "Nowhere is this more clear than in the laws against possession of marijuana in private for personal

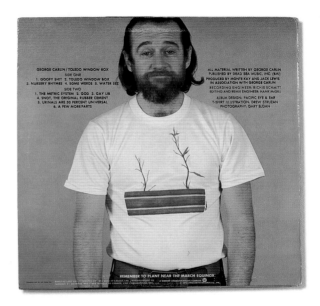

George Carlin's "Toledo Window Box" album graphics with an obviously stoned Carlin don't need much explaining. Nor do the songs which include "Snot, The Original Rubber Cement" and "A Few More Farts."

use." But at the same time a conservative sentiment against the drug was building. Parents and educators were alarmed with high rates of marijuana use among students — one survey found that one-in-twelve high school seniors smoked dope on a daily basis — as the drug slowly moved from a more or less medical concern to a politically charged moral issue.

The governments tried to sort out their budding relationship with pot, but the drug was securing its place in the popular culture. The hippie era

WASH. D.C.
JULY 4
1971 SMOKE
-IN-

Let's twist again like we
did last summer!

paved the way for mellow singer-songwriters like James Taylor and John Denver, who were the aural equivalent of a gentle marijuana buzz, while bands like Pink Floyd and Emerson, Lake and Palmer created intricate, moody albums, perfectly suited to the eager stoner and his stereo headphones. Although they never came out and actually said it, the music industry had discovered that there was money to be made catering to the marijuana generation.

The music world's love affair would reach its zenith in the early 1970s, as reggae music emerged as an international sensation. As the semi-official soundtrack of Jamaica's Rastafarian movement, reggae merged a modern music sensibility with the spiritual vigor of an established African cannabis cult. The Rastafarian movement, formed in the 1930s, considered marijuana, or ganja, a healing sacred herb, and looked to the Bible for its blessings. "He causeth the grass for the cattle, and herb for the service of man." (Psalms 104:14.) They believe "herb" to mean cannabis. Rastas like Bob Marley and the Wailers and Toots and the Maytals sang the praises of cannabis, which had been introduced to the New World in 1492, and reintroduced to the Caribbean in the late 1800s by an influx of workers from the subcontinent.

Things began to turn for the marijuana movement in the mid-1970s. After five years of small victories — culminating in the Alaskan government's 1975 decision to legalize pot — the tide was turning. The summer of 1976 marked a watershed for pot politics. In the lazy heat of an Atlanta August night, Ron and Marsha Manatt watched in distress as a band of sulky teenagers gathered to celebrate their daughter's thirteenth birthday. It's a mystery why they didn't just stop the party then and there and send everyone home without birthday cake. Instead, they stayed out of sight until the last little partygoer staggered home, then went out to the yard to investigate. In the back corner they found empty beer and wine bottles, along with roaches and rolling papers. A few days later, the Manatts started on

Poster for a 1971 Washington Smoke-In (opposite). A poster (below) from NORML, the National Organization for the Reform of Marijuana Laws.

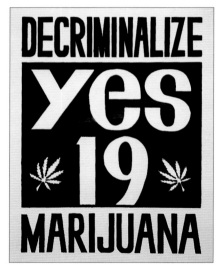

an anti-marijuana crusade which would eventually reach the highest levels of government.

One of the first things Marsha Manatt did was write a letter to Robert DuPont, head of the National Institute on Drug Abuse, a federal agency mainly responsible for drug education. DuPont was struck by Manatt's passion and energy, and asked her to write a parent's guide to marijuana. The result was titled *Parents, Peers, and Pot*. Soon, other parents joined the fight, and eventually formed an anti-pot forum called the National Federation of Parents for Drug Free Youth, or NFP.

The election of conservatives like Ronald Reagan and Margaret Thatcher in the early 1980s further undermined marijuana's standing. Reagan, in particular, was the product of the fifties paranoia that equated

"Penalties against possession of a drug should not be more damaging to an individual than the use of the drug itself." *President Jimmy Carter, August 2, 1977.*

You didn't have to be a pothead to sign a petition to legalize marijuana in 1971, as this hip New Yorker proves (opposite). A poster (above) from the California Marijuana Initiative, late 1972.

marijuana use with communism. This vision meshed nicely with that of the NFP, and he took their call for a drug-free America to heart. The president's wife Nancy became the dowager of the anti-drug movement, and her popular "Just Say No" campaign encouraged teens to avoid pot and other drugs, and employers to root out drug users in their staff. Few people questioned the value of using an elderly millionaire as a role model for streetwise fourteen-year-old potheads and cocaine addicts, but her call for regular urine tests to weed out weedy employees did not go unnoticed. Folk/punk artist Mojo Nixon summed up the mood of the resistance, singing "I ain't going to pee-pee in a cup, unless Nancy Reagan drinks it up."

In 1982, Reagan created a new agency, the White House Drug Abuse

ROLLING along

A collection of vintage and modern rolling-paper packets shows a remarkable diversity of design and color. The papers themselves can be colored or flavored, and are made from a variety of fibers. Originally rolling papers were made from hemp and lately some manufacturers are returning to it as their fiber of choice. There are four basic shapes and sizes of papers, the largest of which is king size — for those 4-inch party joints. One of the oldest rolling-paper manufacturers is the Spanish company Miquel y Costas & Miquel whose "Smoking" papers have been in production since 1876.

Policy Office, a sign that he was taking pot seriously. Over the next six years, Reagan brought back mandatory minimum sentences for drug crimes and sent criminal penalties through the roof. First-time marijuana offenders faced anything from probation to life in prison and could have their property seized indiscriminately; it even became illegal to be caught with pot paraphernalia, anything from roach clips to rolling papers could land you in the slammer. Caught up in the fever, state legislators went wacky on the weed. Eric Schlosser, in his August 1994 *Atlantic Monthly* article "Reefer Madness," noted that by the end of the 1980s, penalties for marijuana convictions varied widely from state to state. "In Montana selling a pound of marijuana, first offense, could lead to a life sentence," Schlosser wrote. "In New Mexico, selling 10,000 pounds of marijuana, first offense, could be

Long before Giorgio Armani began experimenting with hemp fashions, this Italian lady had already devised a stylish way to transport her bundle of hemp fiber.

"Industrial hemp is one of the most important, or at least most promising, new agricultural crops that will make the 21st century a swell time to be alive."

Dr. Alexander Sumach, Director of the Hemp Futures Study Group.

punished with a prison term of no more than three years."

Other countries followed America's weedy lead. Arrest rates for marijuana crimes soared worldwide. Britain alone was putting away more than twenty thousand a year for pot offenses. It had instigated some tough laws, including the 1986 Drug Trafficking Offences Act, which allowed police to confiscate a suspected drug dealer's assets.

In the short term, the anti-marijuana campaign seemed to pay off. Pot use declined throughout the 1980s. But at the same time, the use of hard drugs like cocaine and heroin took off, prompting a frightful rise in inner-city violent crime rates. The problem was that neighborhood pot dealers were scared off by the new rules and regulations, leaving marijuana sales in the hands of career criminals. At that point, simple economics took over. Although the markup for marijuana had always been good, the weed was bulky and difficult to transport. Serious drug dealers preferred to move cocaine or its compact little sister, crack, which yielded a much greater dollar return for virtually the same risk. So criminals moved into crack in a big way.

By the end of the decade, the world's pot policies had regressed. Britain was arresting a record number — more than forty thousand people a year — for cannabis crimes. As for the rest of Europe, Holland remained the only country willing to give pot a chance. In the States, Reagan's successor, George Bush, kept the war on drugs rolling along, and at one point considered closing the country's borders to stem the flow of drugs. Looking back, it's hard to figure out exactly what was going on. Why was the government willing to spend a king's ransom — several thousand kings actually, as some estimates put the costs of the twelve-year war on drugs as high as $3 trillion?

It was the Era of Excess, when the likes of Madonna and Michael Jackson ruled the airwaves, when Trump was teaching us the Art of the Deal, when cocaine was the drug of choice for whoever could afford it, and the collective debt of the Western world was measured in trillions of dollars. Somehow spending a few trillion dollars to rid the world of drugs seemed to make sense. And marijuana, the humble little herb, still lumped in with hard drugs like cocaine, was caught up in the fight.

mythinformation

INDUSTRIAL STRENGTH?

There is lots of talk about how strong marijuana is in the '90s, and that it is much more potent than it was in the past. However, today's marijuana is probably being compared to low-THC marijuana samples from the early '70s. As Lynn Zimmer, Ph.D. and John P. Morgan, M.D., report in *Marijuana Myths, Marijuana Facts*, "Even at that time, the best marijuana was much stronger than the DEA [Drug Enforcement Agency] samples, and it has probably increased in potency since then, though it is nowhere near the 30 to 40 percent THC levels claimed by anti-marijuana propaganda." In any case, even if the marijuana is stronger today, it is probably healthier, say the authors. Less toking is needed to get high and therefore less tar is inhaled into the lungs.

A German poster features a man planting and harvesting marijuana with an ironic reference to a leading German cigarette. Loosely translated: Roll up your sleeves; Plant something yourself; Look forward to the harvest; Smoke Ernte '79; Ernte '79, the pure taste with no additives.

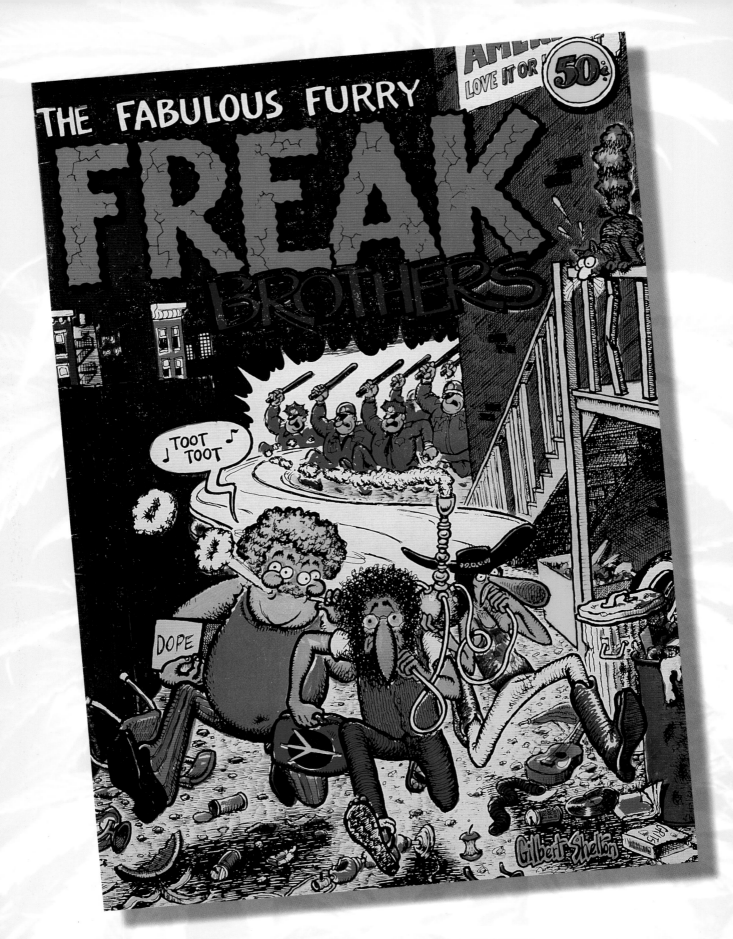

COMIC art

MARIJUANA WAS THE MUSE FOR MANY UNDERGROUND FUNNIES THAT EMERGED IN THE '60s AND '70s.

The late '60s and early '70s were the heyday of underground comics. Here illustrators were free to create satires about the counterculture, and drugs, of course, were part of it. But as Mark James Estren points out in *A History of Underground Comics*, it wasn't always necessary to be stoned to enjoy them. Robert Crumb, the most famous underground cartoonist, creator of Fritz the Cat, the *Zap* and *Snatch* comics, and the *Cheap Thrills* album cover for Big Brother and the Holding Company, drew hiliarious, often sexually charged art. Dope was also one of Crumb's favorite subjects, which he treated with slightly more subtlety than other illustrators of the time. In 1971, he created **HOME GROWN FUNNIES** (first cover right) with such memorable characters as Mary Jane and Kilroy. Crumb now resides in France.

The lovable **FABULOUS FURRY FREAK BROTHERS** (left), created by Gilbert Shelton and first published in a comic book with Rip Off Press in 1970, are the stoned equivalent of the Keystone Cops. Constantly involved in one zany adventure after another, usually involving drugs, the Freak Brothers are still alive and kicking in the '90s.

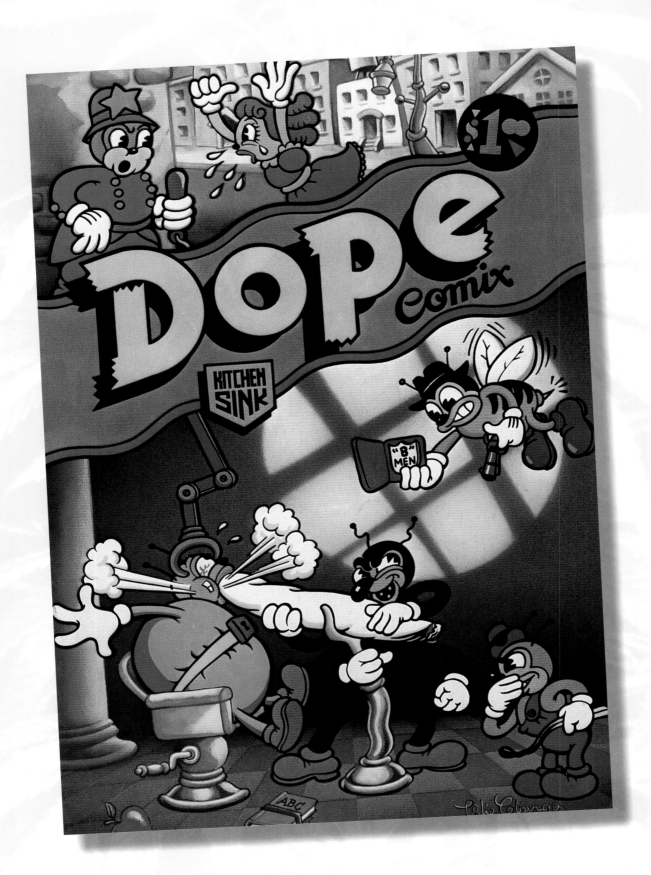

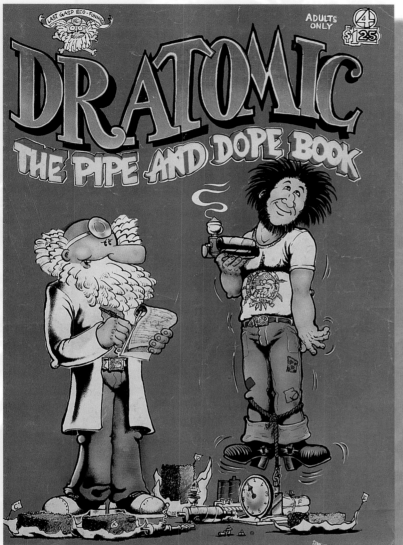

In fact, in *The Adventures of Mavrides and Shelton*, the brothers are judges of fine connoisseur pot at the 3rd Annual *High Times* Cannabis Cup in Amsterdam (see page 138).

The first cover for **DOPE COMIX** (far left), published by Kitchen Sink Press, was more obvious than others in its reference to drugs. Drawn by Leslie Cabarga, who is probably most famous for reviving Betty Boop, it resembles the style of the Fleischer Brothers, creators of Betty. Kitchen Sink Press, founded and edited by Denis Kitchen, published underground comics for 30 years before going out of business in 1999.

Larry Todd drew the covers for the six **DR. ATOMIC** comics published by Last Gasp Publishing. Cover Number 4 (left). The first cover for **TOONEY LOONS AND MARIJUANA MELODIES** (below) by Kenneth P. Greene.

CHAPTER SEVEN

Fields of Dreams

CANNABIS GROWS UP IN THE '90s

THE CONSERVATIVE ATTACK on marijuana had done the trick. By the time the 1990s rolled around, weed was on the decline, with jails overflowing with dazed and confused potheads who barely knew what hit them. But as cannabis entered the 1990s on the edge of extinction, it somehow emerged near the end of the decade on the verge of distinction.

"The drug is really quite a remarkably safe one for humans, although it is really quite a dangerous one for mice and they should not use it."

J.W.D. Henderson, Director of the Bureau of Human Drugs, Health and Welfare Canada, speaking about marijuana. From High Society, *by Neil Boyd.*

Europe led the way for the cannabis comeback. The whiff that something was in the air almost passed by unnoticed. In Britain, Opposition Labour MP and future prime minister Tony Blair publicly called for the legalization of pot, and a few months later, in February of 1992, the U.K. government announced a plan to grant licenses for hemp farmers and medical researchers, and the governments of Canada and Australia soon followed suit. Not long afterwards, representatives from seventeen prominent European cities met in Frankfurt, Germany, to sign a charter supporting recreational marijuana use. From then on it seemed cannabis couldn't keep itself out of the news. First the German High Court deemed the criminalization of cannabis unconstitutional, then the first hemp fashions rolled into the boutiques on London's trendy streets. By now, even the Americans were getting into the act, as president-elect Bill Clinton caused an uproar by announcing that he'd once smoked, but not inhaled, pot.

A lush hemp field (opposite) in Manitoba, Canada, was seeded only a month earlier. Label for the first Canadian hemp beer (below) from a Vancouver microbrewery.

123

"I did not inhale." *Bill Clinton in 1992.*

In light of all this positive press, it's hard to believe that everyone wasn't jumping on the hemp-powered bandwagon. But in many cases it was business as usual for the actual powers that be. In France, the government flat out rejected the recommendation of its own Henrion Commission, which called for a two-year pilot project to test the feasibility of a domestic retail pot industry. Meanwhile, in England, as MPs were calling for the legalization of pot in Parliament, Home Secretary Michael Howard increased the fines for cannabis possession, and police forces were arresting a record number of Britain's cannabis criminals. Even Holland has not been immune to pressure. In 1997, as Europe moved toward union, other countries began to worry that Holland's liberal drug policies would spread. The Dutch reluctantly made some concessions: they reduced the number of coffee shops allowed to sell drugs, raised the minimum buying age from sixteen to eighteen, and restricted purchase quantities. Despite the concessions, the Dutch maintain that their drug experiment has been a success, pointing out that their recreational drug consumption per capita was the lowest in Europe.

In the U.S., in 1997, approximately 700,000 people were arrested for marijuana-related offenses. That same year, Congress began deliberations on a little legal ditty called the Drug Importer Death Penalty Act. Proposed by former House Speaker Newt Gingrich — who admitted to smoking the herb himself in his wild and woolly college years — it called for life in prison with no chance of parole to any first offender convicted of importing a little less than two ounces of marijuana into the country. Even without the official Death Penalty Act, experience has proved time and time again that the biggest risk to a marijuana user's health and well-being is not the drug, but the laws in place to prohibit its use. In one case, in 1992, Donald Scott was shot to death by police who raided his Malibu, California, ranch in search of pot plants. None were found.

Bill Clinton (opposite) tries to keep things straight. An English bobby searches pot protester (below).

125

Meanwhile, the return of mandatory minimum sentences meant marijuana offenders often earned lengthier jail terms than armed robbers, murderers, and rapists, as the sad story of Mark Young bears witness. In 1992, Young was sentenced to life in prison for conspiring to sell marijuana. The fact that Young had merely introduced a marijuana farmer to a potential buyer bore no weight in court. Undoubtedly, the government had hoped to make an example of Young and his Indiana co-conspirators. The Midwest had become a hotbed of marijuana farming, which makes sense. Cannabis and corn thrive under the exact same growing conditions; but while a bushel of corn can bring a hardworking farmer two or three dollars at market, a bushel of cut-and-dried marijuana buds can net in the neighborhood of $50,000. That's a nice neighborhood, compared to where your average farmer lives. It seems that times had changed. In the 1960s and 1970s, most of America's marijuana was imported from Mexico and Jamaica, but by the nineties, homegrown cannabis was a hot — by some estimates, the hottest — cash crop in the country, with annual profits estimated at several hundred million dollars.

The Body Shop, with a slogan of "It's hope not dope," launched hemp-based products in 1998.

And there lies the secret to the cannabis comeback. In the early 1990s, American business people were waking up to the fact that the greeny green and greenback go hand in hand. Not only were the people for pot, but governments were losing millions and millions of tax dollars each year on illegally grown marijuana — not to mention spending anywhere from $8 billion to $15 billion on anti-marijuana law enforcement programs. And hemp fabric had come back big time. In 1993, retailers around the world sold about $5 million of hemp-based products; two years later, that figure had risen to $75 million. As the millennium comes to a close, annual sales of hemp approach the $200-million mark.

126

Fashion maestro Giorgio Armani combined his elegant fashion sensibility with an ecological philosophy when he included hemp in his 1997 Emporio Armani collection. He used the venerable fabric in jeans, skirts, and jackets. Armani continued using hemp in these bowls (below) made for the 1998 Emporio Armani Gift Collection.

Please keep off the grass

No matter what side of the marijuana debate you're on, most people agree that adolescence, already a confusing time for most kids, is made more complicated by smoking marijuana. As Senator Tom Hayden said in *Time* magazine, "Marijuana has never improved anyone's ability to do homework or hit a curve ball." A young smoker (right) gets high at a 1996 pro-pot rally in Boston.

GROWING trends

In the last 30 years marijuana growers have become artisans of cultivation, developing new strains with specialized properties and refining old favorites.

As a wine connoisseur can admire the taste of a finely crafted grape, so too can a seasoned cannabis smoker appreciate differences in taste and delicate nuances of intoxication. The best pot is smooth, burns evenly, and has a musky, pungent aroma, not unlike the smoke of an aromatic pipe tobacco. Different types of pot enchant the mind and body in varying degrees and forms. One type of stone sharpens the senses while another dulls them. Some pot "creeps up on you," while other varieties bend the mind from the very first draw.

The number of different types of marijuana available today is truly staggering considering possession of the plant is illegal in most parts of the world. Nonetheless, the marketplace demands choice and whether it's "Pearly Girl," "Hindu Kush," or "Iggy," the consumer gets what they want in the end.

Hindu Kush

Hemp Star

Big Bud

Pearly Girl

Shiskaberry

Jack Herer

Iggy

Canadian Ross Rebagliati is reinstated as gold medalist in snowboarding at the Nagano Olympics in 1998. Rebagliati, who had been disqualified when traces of marijuana were detected in his body, claimed he inhaled secondhand smoke at a farewell party.

In an age where consumers are much more environmentally aware, hemp makes sense. It's still the most durable natural fiber around. A pair of jeans or a shirt made from hemp will last twice as long as cotton or wool. Meanwhile, the same qualities that made hemp valuable during yesterday's Age of Sails — its inherent strength and versatility — make it perfect for today's Age of Sales. Home furnishings like carpeting, window coverings, bedding, and furniture are perfectly suited to hemp fiber. Even the pulp and paper industry is beginning to use hemp, as the world looks to find a high-yielding, dependable paper source. While a harvested forest takes around forty years to recover, hemp is an annual crop. Moreover, hemp makes very

"In the absence of clear regulations about marijuana use at the Olympics, Mr. Rebagliati was sensibly allowed to keep his medal in the end. But his reverse-Clinton defense — he inhaled, but didn't smoke — deserved a separate medal for cheekiness." New York Times *editorial, February 14, 1998.*

little waste: the stalks are used for fiber, the flowers for medicine, and the seeds for oil and food — cannabis seeds are an easy digestible protein.

Hemp's cause got a boost from an unexpected source: a real live Hollywood celebrity. In 1996, Woody Harrelson, who'd made a name for himself as the lovable barkeep hick on TV's "Cheers," planted four certified industrial hemp seeds on his property in rural Lee County, Kentucky. It was a simple act that could have landed the actor up to three months in jail. Harrelson wanted to test state laws which did not recognize the difference between cannabis grown for hemp fiber and cannabis grown for marijuana. "We are facing a severe worldwide fiber shortage," Harrelson told the press at the time of his arrest. "Industrial hemp can help meet our fiber needs while also revitalizing our struggling rural economies."

Harrelson's dramatic display put him, and hemp, in the media spotlight across the country. Meanwhile, his court challenge made waves. In two trials, judges ruled in his favor; the courts agreed that the state failed to make a proper distinction between hemp and marijuana. Harrelson is not the only one to challenge the current laws. Canadian Chris Clay, who admitted selling a cannabis seedling in 1997, sought to have the law outlawing the non-commercial trafficking of marijuana ruled void. Clay maintained the law violated his rights under Canada's *Charter of Rights and Freedoms*. After a lengthy trial that included the benefits of medicinal marijuana, Clay was convicted of trafficking in a narcotic. He is appealing his conviction. Two years later, a Toronto social activist suffering from AIDS won the right to legally grow and smoke marijuana for medicinal purposes. The Ontario Supreme

MURPHY BROWN TAKES A HIT Medical use of marijuana got a big boost from fictional anchorwoman Murphy Brown (opposite) who finished her eleventh year of the popular U.S. television sitcom with cancer and marijuana. It's the first time in North American television history that a sitcom character is shown smoking dope for medical reasons. In one of the final episodes of the long-running series entitled "Waiting to Inhale," Murphy's friend and co-anchor, Jim Dial, scores her a bag of dope. Jim, who smokes with Murphy on the episode — and subsequently forgets her name as he becomes stoned — wanted to help relieve his friend's suffering from the side effects of her breast cancer treatments.

Court agreed with Jim Wakeford that his civil rights had been violated.

The medical marijuana question was not a new one. Back in the 1930s, doctors were the first outspoken opponents of Harry Anslinger and his Marihuana Tax Act. More recently, the debate has been heating up. In 1978, New Mexico became the first state to legally recognize marijuana's treatment potential after cancer patient Lynn Pierson brought his story to the state legislator. He told his government that he used marijuana to help deal with the symptoms of his cancer treatment. In light of his case, the governor called for a public hearing. After testimony from cancer and glaucoma patients, with support from the doctors who treat them, the legislature gave physicians the power to prescribe pot when needed. Unfortunately, Pierson didn't live to see this outcome. He died in August 1978. Over the next ten years, the federal government initiated the Compassionate Investigative New Drug Program, which allowed family doctors to ask for special permission to offer marijuana as a treatment option to specific patients. But in 1988, the anti-drug Bush administration suspended the program. Since

then, groups representing patients and their physicians have put more and more pressure on governments to relax medical marijuana laws, and one by one, states have begun to fall into line. In 1996, California voters passed Proposition 215, allowing patients medical access to marijuana, with Arizona and Massachusetts enacting similar laws a year later.

To date, twenty-six states and the District of Columbia have passed measures allowing doctors to prescribe pot. At the same time, governments in Britain, Canada, Germany, France, and Australia are exploring the use of

"I'd always done a lot of glue as a kid. I was very interested in glue, and then I went to lager and speed, and I drifted into heroin because as a kid growing up everybody told me, 'Don't smoke marijuana, it will kill you.'"

Irvine Welsh, author of the best-selling novel about heroin addiction, Trainspotting.

cannabis to treat patients. Even bonny Prince Charles got into the act. At a visit to a day-treatment center in London, the Prince suggested to a multiple-sclerosis patient that she try pot to relieve her pain. The move toward medical marijuana is based on research which shows that marijuana is an effective treatment in numerous medical conditions. Today, cancer patients smoke pot to relieve vomiting and other problems associated with chemotherapy, and people suffering from AIDS take marijuana to stimulate their appetite; in fact, in many cancer clinics and AIDS hospices, there are designated areas for patients who want to smoke up. Other treatment applications include afflictions of the central nervous system, such as multiple sclerosis, where marijuana reduces pain and muscle spasms, and epilepsy, where the drug helps patients ward off seizures.

Of course, the drug is not without its risks. Smoke is smoke and chronic long-term marijuana smokers do face respiratory problems. Although Britain's prestigious medical journal *The Lancet* gave long-term use of the weed a clean bill of health in its November 11, 1995 editorial, three years later they admitted that "chronic heavy cannabis smoking is associated with increased symptoms of chronic bronchitis, such as coughing, production of sputum, and wheezing." In *Marijuana Myths, Marijuana Facts*, authors Lynn

Zimmer, Ph.D., and John P. Morgan, M.D., acknowledge that "this is the one well-established physical risk associated with marijuana use by otherwise healthy adults: heavy pot smoking can aggravate chronic respiratory disease." However, used in moderation, marijuana smoke does not appear to be dangerous. "Although it contains roughly the same quantity of carcinogens as tobacco," the authors go on to state, "when used on its own, without tobacco, marijuana has never been known to cause lung cancer." (See sidebar Is Pot Bad For You? page 144.)

With all the positive press cannabis has been getting lately, it's no surprise that recreational use of marijuana is on the rise. Coincidentally, pot has once again made its way into pop culture. Although it's a long way from the days when Cheech and Chong would include a giant rolling paper in their records, young people today are listening to hip hop and rap artists extolling the virtues of pot, and immersing themselves in a retro-disco seventies scene that makes pot cool again. While some parents and politicians might not like what they see — and smell — it appears that pot has found its place.

A high-tech greenhouse for Sensi Seeds, a seed-breeding company in the Netherlands, produces seeds that are sold all over the world.

DUTCH treats

Welcome to the Cannabis Cup. Each year pot aficionados make a pilgrimage to Amsterdam, where they get to sample and judge the world's best marijuana and hash. The annual convention now in its eleventh year is the brainchild of American magazine *High Times*. More than 1,500 people, including your average pothead as well as celebrity judges from around the world, register for the week long event, which features prizes for categories that include best coffee shop, best homegrown pot, and best imported hash.

In 1997, the Cannabis Cup featured the first Hall of Fame award, which was given posthumously to Bob Marley. Rita Marley was there to pick up the honors.

And just like any other convention, there are reps for companies selling everything from the latest in bongs to other drug paraphernalia. There's even some serious discussions about enviromental, political, and medical concerns, but most people are there for another kind of buzz.

The Adventures of Mavrides and Shelton *(above)*.
A joint prepared with "Orange Bud," a legendary strain, is a welcome sight at the Homegrown Fantasy coffee shop (opposite). (Overleaf) Later that day, at the opening night ceremonies of the Cannabis Cup, High Times *editor, Steve Bloom (middle), and friends burn the midnight spliff.*

A "vaporizer" unit (opposite) is used to obtain a clean, potent high at the Sensi Seeds booth. Cup delegates sample four to five varieties a day; a vote follows at week's end. Johan Dieke (top), pot-tender at the De Rokerij coffee shop, smells the sweet essence of a cannabis plant on display. Two of the staff (above left) at De Rokerij coffee shop display their wares. At the end of the week-long cannabis fest a delighted delegate (above right) empties the trophy case of the best hash and pot available in Holland.

IS POT
bad for you?

There's good news for moderate smokers in the latest research on marijuana and bad news for heavy smokers. Getting caught or causing an accident while stoned are still the greatest dangers, but those who smoke marijuana on a weekly or daily basis over several years risk potentially serious damage to some mental faculties and to their lungs. Adolescents who are heavy pot smokers may retard their emotional and intellectual development.

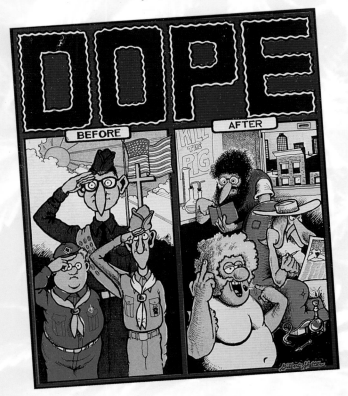

balance. Until recently, no one understood how marijuana penetrates the brain.

Then, in 1992, a Hebrew University team discovered chemicals in the brain that are similar to cannabinoids, the class of chemicals contained in marijuana. These newly discovered chemicals, called anandamides, may block pain and help regular sleep patterns. THC (delta-9-tetrahydrocannabinol), the marijuana ingredient most responsible for altering consciousness, uses the same docking station in brain cells as anandamides do. Pot defender Dr. John P. Morgan, co-author of *Marijuana Myths, Marijuana Facts*, says that THC merely "borrows a prepared pathway"; that is, it makes use of a functioning system without contaminating it. Pot foe, Dr. Robert DuPont, former head of the National Institute on Drug Abuse, says that THC "pirates" the brain's communication network. By that, DuPont means that pot users are allowing THC to steal cell receptors that should be used only by the brain's chemicals and are risking permanent changes to the brain.

1 HOW DOES POT WORK?

Pot creates a high by affecting strategic locations in the brain, including the hippocampus, where linear thinking takes place; the rostral ventromedial medulla, at the base of the brain, which modulates the intensity of pain sensations; and the cerebellum, which coordinates movement and

2 DOES POT MAKE YOU STUPID?

Repeated studies of long-term, heavy pot smokers in Costa Rica have yielded no convincing evidence that smokers are slower thinkers than nonsmokers. And Dr. Andrew Weil, author of the first double-blind human experiments with marijuana, in 1968, contends that "whatever changes may occur in mental function associated with marijuana use, they will all reverse if you get people away from it." However, studies in India, Europe and the U.S. have found that heavy use brings an increased risk of potentially permanent short-term-memory loss and may hinder the ability to adapt to new rules and situations.

While the question of whether or not pot inflicts permanent damage remains unresolved, scientists agree that pot has temporary cognitive effects. In a recent study, researchers at McLean Hospital, in Belmont, Massachusetts, found that mental function in heavy users was inhibited for twenty-four hours after subjects had smoked pot, long after the high was gone. If you smoke pot regularly and don't notice any problems, then you may not be suffering any damage at all — or you may have adjusted to a lower intellectual standard.

3 CAN POT HOOK YOU?

Marijuana has been ranked with caffeine in addictiveness potential — considerably lower than alcohol, nicotine or cocaine. About one in every eleven people who try pot becomes a chronic, heavy user for a time. Most seem able to stop at will. Those who do become dependent on marijuana sometimes undergo a form of withdrawal when they abstain. A credible study by psychiatrists at the University of California at San Diego documented withdrawal symptoms in about sixteen percent of their study subjects, who had all used pot daily for an average of almost seventy months. These symptoms included nervousness, tension, restlessness, sleep disturbance and appetite changes.

"Smoking pot every third Saturday night isn't going to damage you in any measurable way, unless you do something stupid when you're stoned," says Mark Kleiman, a drug policy expert at the University of California at Los Angeles. The hidden risk is that "you won't be able to keep it to every third Saturday night."

4 DOES POT HURT YOUR LUNGS?

Marijuana smoke contains many of the same toxic chemicals as tobacco smoke, including carcinogens such as tar, carbon monoxide and cyanide. Occasional pot users do not generally inhale enough smoke to affect the linings of the trachea and bronchial tubes. Heavy users, however, often experience the respiratory problems that pack-a-day cigarette smokers do, such as chronic bronchitis and exacerbation of asthma.

The largest cohort of people using pot on a regular, long-term basis in the U.S. began smoking in the sixties, so they haven't yet reached the age when cancers manifest with a vengeance. Small-scale studies of chronic pot users' lungs have revealed abnormal changes in bronchial cells, indicating an increased risk of cancer, and many scientists believe that pot's lung-cancer risk could prove to be comparable to that of cigarettes.

5 CAN POT CURE A HEADACHE?

"In the 1970s and 1980s, drug companies such as Eli Lilly were very excited about the medical uses of marijuana," says Dr. John Morgan, "before the War on Drugs escalated and they gave up." One of the exciting discoveries in pot research — most of which is being conducted in Europe — is that cannabinoids probably have pain-killing properties; there are some reports that they could be useful in alleviating migraines. They also may work as antioxidants, thus reducing brain swelling in stroke and head-trauma victims. Pot is now used regularly — often illegally — to reduce the need for morphine, to counteract nausea and to stimulate appetite in people with wasting diseases like AIDS.

Hemp in outer space?

WHAT DOES THE future hold for the humble cannabis plant? Without question, hemp-based products will continue to rack up sales. Already hemp is a key ingredient in everything from jeans and backpacks, to wrapping paper and tablecloths, to cologne and aftershave and shampoo and lip balm — there's even hemp beer, if you're so inclined.

No doubt, as both the commercial and medical acceptance of cannabis grows, governments will rethink their legal opposition to recreational use of marijuana. Right now, most countries in the West take a fairly benign approach to the drug. The Canadian Association of Chiefs of Police called for the decriminalization of marijuana in April, 1999. Australia, Belgium, Britain, Denmark, France, Italy, Germany, Luxembourg, Spain, Switzerland, Portugal — all take a fairly lax view of casual cannabis use, although it's still technically illegal. Likewise, many of these countries are allowing their farmers to try their hand at hemp husbandry, and cannabis accounts for one of the few growth areas in the agricultural industry today. The last bastion is the United States, where laws remain harsher than a Wisconsin winter. But change will come, as the dollars start to make sense.

So hang on to your hemp hats. The marijuana millennium is dawning as cannabis, the little plant that could, is set to prove that the first ten thousand years were no fluke. Like rock 'n' roll, death and taxes, the plucky cannabis plant is here to stay and ready to resume its place as the world's favorite weed.

A new strain from California, "Juicy Fruit," (opposite) is a favorite among people using marijuana for medical reasons.

Recommended Reading

Artificial Paradise
by Charles Baudelaire
A Citadel Press Book
Carol Publishing Group, 1996

Atlantic Monthly
"Reefer Madness" and "Marijuana and the
Law" by Eric Schlosser
August 1994 and September 1994

The Great Book of Hemp
by Rowan Robinson
Park Street Press, a division of
Inner Traditions International, 1996

Hashish!
by Robert Connell Clarke
Red Eye Press Inc., 1998

Hep-Cats, Narcs, and Pipe Dreams
A History of America's Romance with
Illegal Drugs
by Jill Jonnes
Scribner, 1996

High Society
Legal and Illegal Drugs in Canada
by Neil Boyd
Key Porter Books, 1991

A History of Underground Comics
by Mark James Estren
Straight Arrow Books, 1974

Marihuana Reconsidered
by Lester Grinspoon, M.D.
Quick American Archives, 1994

Marihuana: The First Twelve Thousand Years
by Ernest Abel
Plenum Press, 1980

Marihuana, the Forbidden Medicine
by Lester Grinspoon, M.D., and
James B. Bakalar
Yale University Press, 1993

Marijuana Myths, Marijuana Facts
by Lynn Zimmer, Ph.D., and
John P. Morgan, M.D.
Lindesmith Center, 1997

Opium: A History
by Martin Booth
A Thomas Dunne Book
St. Martin's Press, 1996

Plants of the Gods: Origins of Hallucinogenic Use
by Richard Evans Schultes and Albert Hofman
McGraw-Hill Book Company, 1979

Reefer Madness
Marijuana in America
by Larry Solman
Grove Press, 1979

Romancing Mary Jane
A Year in the Life of a Failed Marijuana Grower
by Michael Poole
Greystone Books, a division of Douglas
& McIntyre Ltd., 1998

Tales of Hashish
A Literary Look at the Hashish Experience
Edited and annotated by Andrew C. Kimmens
William Morrow and Company, Inc., 1977

A Treasury of Hashish
by Dr. Alexander Sumach
Stoneworks, 1975

Waiting for the Man
The Story of Drugs and Popular Music
by Harry Shapiro
Quartet Books, 1988

Index

F

G

H

Contributors

Jeff Canja
Modern Age Books
P.O. Box 325
East Lansing, Michigan
48826
517/487-9313

Chris Clay
c/o The Organic Traveller
see right

The Friendly Stranger
226 Queen St. West
Toronto, Ontario
M5V 1Z6
416/591-1570

Matthijs T. Huijgen
HempWorld, Inc.
http://www.Hemp-CyberFarm.com
http://www.HempHotel.com

Bob Kennedy
Envirohemp
509 Bloor St. West
Toronto, Ontario
M5F 1Y2
416/413-7758

Marijuana and Hemp History
Museum and Library
see The Organic Traveller
Curator: Peter Young

Terry Nudds
Science Fiction/Fantasy/Horror/Pulps
email: tnudds@worldchat.com
http://www.abebooks.com/home/lostlibrary/

The Organic Traveller
101-343 Richmond St.
London, Ontario
N6A 3C2
Phone: 519/432-HEMP
Fax: 519/432-1618

Roll Your Own
43 Melville Avenue
Toronto, Ontario
M6G 1Y1
1-888-476-5543
http://www.roll-your-own.com

Leonard Shoup
Pulp Books
email: lshoup@worldchat.com
http://www.abebooks.com/home/elder gods/

John Silverstein
Hot Property
416/538-2127
email: hotprop@interlog.com

Dr. Alexander Sumach
author *A Treasury of Hashish* and
Director of the Hemp Futures Study Group,
Niagara-on-the-Lake, Ontario

Joe Wein
Hemp in Japan
http://www.taima.org

Credits

FOREWORD. Page 8: André Grossman; page 9: Hunt Institute for Botanical Documentation, Carnegie Mellon University, Pittsburgh, PA.

CHAPTER ONE. Page 12: Kichijo-ten by anonymous (8th century), Yakushi-ji Temple, Nara, Japan (photo by Asukaen Co., Ltd.); page 14: Head of Buddha, India, 2nd century (schist), Fitzwilliam Museum, University of Cambridge, UK/Bridgeman Art Library, London/New York; page 15: The Gutenberg Bible, Mainz c. 1450-55, Christie's Images/Bridgeman Art Library, London/New York; page 16: "Lady emerges from her moskito (sic) net," by Hokkei, Private Collection; page 19: Lovers standing in a palace pavilion, their legs supported on long cushions, Rajasthan, c. 1750, (gouache on paper), Private Collection/Bridgeman Art Library, London/New York; page 20: The family of Shiva, from the 'Rang Mahal Chamba,' Chamba, Himachal Pradesh, Pahari School, 1840, (mural), National Museum of India, New Delhi, India/Bridgeman Art Library, London/New York; page 22: (top) Blair McKinnon; (bottom) André Grossman.

CHAPTER TWO. Page 24: *La Servante de Harem* (1874) by Paul-Désiré Trouillebert, Musée des Beaux-Arts de Nice, France (photo by Michel de Lorenzo); page 27: *Allumeuse de Narghilé* (1898) by Jean-Léon Gérôme, Gallery Keops, Geneva; pages 28/29: *English Ships and the Spanish Armada*, 1588, English School circa 16th century, © National Maritime Museum Picture Library, U.K.; page 31: *Life of George Washington, The Farmer*, hand-colored lithograph by Claude Regnier after the painting by Junius Brutus Stearns, Library of Congress, Washington; page 33: Thomas Jefferson as Minister to France — 1784 to 1789, woodcut by Charles

Turzak, 1936, Library of Congress, Washington; pages 34/35: Napoleon Bonaparte (1769-1821) Celebrating the Birthday of the Prophet Mohammed during his campaign on Egypt (1798-1801), engraving by A. Colin (18th century), Private Collection/Roger-Viollet, Paris/Bridgeman Art Library, London/New York.

CHAPTER THREE. Page 36: Baudelaire, self-portrait, circa 1844, watercolor, Collection of Baronne de Goldschmidt-Rothschild, Paris; page 37: *The Hasheesh Eaters* by Honoré Daumier, lithograph, 1845; page 40: The Young Queen Victoria (1819-1901) (panel) by Franz Xavier Winterhalter (1806-73) (circle of) Philip Mould, Historical Portraits Ltd., London, U.K./Bridgeman Art Library, London/New York; page 41: Portrait of Sir William Brooke O'Shaughnessy with his telegraph machine by Hudson Benjamin, Christie's Images Ltd., 1999; pages 42/43: *The Coffee Shop of Cairo* (1849) by David Roberts, R.A. (1796-1864), Victoria and Albert Museum; page 44: photo of William Butler Yeats (1865-1939), The Hulton Getty Picture Collection; page 45: illustration of Maud Gonne Macbride b.1866, The Hulton Getty Picture Collection; page 48: ©Arthur Rackham illustration from *Alice In Wonderland*, reproduced with the kind permission of his family; page 50: *Cannabis sativa L.* illustration courtesy of Hunt Institute for Botanical Documentation, Carnegie Mellon University, Pittsburgh, PA.

CHAPTER FOUR. Page 52: Corbis/Bettman-UPI; page 53: cartoon by Oliver Hereford from *Life*, June 26, 1919, Library of Congress, Washington; pages 54/55: Bain collection, Library of Congress, Washington; page 56: Library of Congress,

Washington; page 57: Library of Congress, Washington; page 58: photo courtesy of The American Heritage Center, University of Wyoming; page 61: Library of Congress, Washington; page 62: Library of Congress, Washington; page 63: Library of Congress, Washington; page 64: engraving from *The Illustrated Police News*, December 2, 1876; page 67: Archive Photos; page 68: *Reefer Madness* poster, courtesy of NORML; pages 68/69: National Archives, Washington; page 71: collection of the Henry Ford Museum & Greenfield Village; page 72: Marijuana and Hemp Museum and Library; page 73: National Archives, Washington; pages 74/75: National Archives, Washington.

CHAPTER FIVE. Page 80: The Allen Ginsberg Trust; page 81: Library of Congress, Washington; page 82: The Hulton Getty Picture Collection; pages 84/85: Wisconsin Center for Film and Theater Research, University of Wisconsin-Madison; page 87: Library of Congress, Washington; page 89: Archive Photos; page 90: The Hulton Getty Picture Collection; page 91: Archive Photos; pages 92/93: National Archives, Washington; page 95: Library of Congress, Washington; page 97: Ralph Crane/LIFE Magazine © Time Inc.; page 98: The Allen Ginsberg Trust; page 99: Charles Harbutt/Actuality Inc.; pages 100/101: Eden Hash posters, Bernard Eisenweiss, Sydney, Australia; page 101: Nepalese hashish, photo by Barge.

CHAPTER SIX. Page 102: Archive Photos; page 103: Marijuana and Hemp History Museum and Library; page 104, Jorge Cervantes; page 105: CP Picture Archive; pages 106-107: Marijuana and Hemp History Museum and Library; pages 108, 109, 110: posters from the Yanker Poster Collection, Library of Congress, Washington; page 111: Archive Photos;

page 114: Francesco Ciapanna; page 117: poster from the Yanker Poster Collection, Library of Congress, Washington; Pages 118 and 144: Front and back cover of "The Collected Adventures of the Fabulous Furry Freak Brothers," published by Rip Off Press Inc., in San Francisco, © 1971 by Gilbert Shelton; pages 119 and 160: © R. Crumb; page 120: Reprinted with permission of Kitchen Sink Press © Leslie Cabarga; page 121: (top) Reprinted with permission of Last Gasp Publishing © Larry Todd; (bottom) © Kenneth P. Greene.

CHAPTER SEVEN. Page 122: Michael Grandmaison, Winnipeg, Manitoba; page 123: label courtesy of The Bowen Island Brewing Co.; page 124: CP Picture Archive (Paul Chiasson); page 125: Jorge Cervantes; page 126: ad courtesy of The Body Shop; page 127: photos courtesy of Emporio Armani; pages 128/129: Brooks Kraft/Sygma; pages 130/131: photos by Barge; page 132: CP Picture Archive (Peter Dejong); page 135: CBS Photo Archive; page 137: Jorge Cervantes; page 138: "The Adventures of Mavrides and Shelton" by Shelton and Mavrides. Published in *High Times* Magazine, November, 1990. © 1990 by Rip Off Press, Inc., © 1996 by Gilbert Shelton; pages 139-143: photos by Bryce Duffy; page 144: see page 118.

AFTERWORD. Page 146: André Grossman.

Photos of printed ephemera pages 72, 76-79, 96, 103, 106-107, 112-113, 118-121, 138, 144: Andrea Emard Photography.

For further information about the Fabulous Furry Freak Brothers go to www.ripoffpress.com. The Fabulous Furry Freak Brothers will soon come to your movie theater as a major, fully animated, motion picture.

Acknowledgments

Many many collectors opened their archives to us and we sincerely thank them (for a complete listing, see pages 157-159).

For copyediting thanks to Bernice Eisenstein; for photo research, Carina Dvorak in Europe, and Margaret Johnson in the U.S.

For advice, translations, and memorabilia thanks to Winston Collins, Stephen Cope, Joseph Gisini, Daphne Hart, Roddy Heading, Bob Kennedy, Dana Larsen, Marcella Saint Amant, Barbara Sears, John Silverstein, Joe Wein, Xavier, Pete Young, and Alan S. Zweig.

Thanks to the following libraries in Toronto who were extremely helpful and patient with all our queries: curator Mariko Liliefeldt and The Japan Foundation Toronto Library; the staff at the H.N. Pullar Library, The Metropolitan Toronto Reference Library, The Museum for Textiles, The Osborne Collection, and Thomas Fisher Rare Book Library.

Also thanks to Stephanie Adams and Erika Fortgang at *Rolling Stone*, George Agostino, Patrick Dowers, Jamie Fraser, Mark Held, and Bruce Pomerantz.

For other contributors, addresses, web sites, and phone numbers, see page 157.

For recommended reading, see page 148.